PRAISE FOR *THE NEW ALPHA*

A field guide for leaders who aspire to be a force for good. It's full of hands-on tools, skill-building exercises, self-assessments, and progress trackers that you can use immediately.

—ADAM GRANT, Wharton professor and *New York Times* bestselling author of *Originals* and *Give and Take*

The traditional "Alpha" concept of leadership is so yesterday, and no one knows that better than Danielle Harlan, purveyor of the brilliant "New Alpha" paradigm. To read Harlan is to take the hand of a wise and friendly coach who believes in you and wants to help you get wherever it is you want to go. Readers emerge knowing how to cultivate the essential habits that will transform us as humans and as leaders, and we're eager to get started *now*. Transcending gender, race, and generation, *The New Alpha* paradigm is a must-read for anyone who longs to unlock their potential and make a significant difference in our world.

—JULIE LYTHCOTT-HAIMS, author, *New York Times* bestseller *How to Raise an Adult*

The New Alpha provides an invaluable road map for those aspiring to be the leaders our society desperately needs—people who strive to be their best selves and to lead with and through others in pursuit of improving our collective welfare.

—WENDY KOPP, founder, Teach For America, and CEO and cofounder, Teach For All

My former college classmate, Danielle Harlan, takes a fascinating deep dive into what motivates today's leaders. It's not just about the skills, energy, and drive to excel, but also a genuine desire to cultivate the best in those they lead to move toward a greater good, a better world. This is an engaging, inspirational read.

—CONGRESSMAN ERIC SWALWELL

The New Alpha is more contemporary and more innovative than any other leadership book I've read. I envision companies scrapping their tired, marginally effective leader development workshops and instead using *The New Alpha* to engage and develop their high potentials.

—Tom Kolditz, PhD, executive director, Ann and John Doerr Institute for New Leaders; Brigadier General, US Army (ret); and founding director, West Point Leadership Center

The New Alpha is fierce! This is not one of your run-of-the-mill aspirational, feel-good, lofty books about leadership. It's a gritty journey through personal reflection and introspection that pushes you out of your comfort zone and propels you into a space where you can transform and redefine parts of yourself to become the "whole" leader and change agent you want to be in every facet of your life and as far- and wide-reaching as you can imagine. If you want to be good, do good, and effect real change in today's world, *The New Alpha* is a must-read!

—Jamila M. Hall, partner, Jones Day, Leadership Atlanta, Class of 2017

Wow! You get your money's worth with Harlan—really, more like three books combined into one. The focus on "personal excellence" would have been more than sufficient, but then Harlan gives this context in terms of making a difference ("personal leadership"), and then application for more effective "team and organizational leadership." Indeed, Harlan understands that, as the airlines instruct, when something unexpected happens you have to put the oxygen mask on yourself before you can help others. If you want to make a difference in your organization, and be an exemplary leader, you have to start with becoming the best you can be.

—Barry Z. Posner, PhD, Accolti Professor of Leadership, Santa Clara University and coauthor of *The Leadership Challenge* and *Learning Leadership*

I loved every page of *The New Alpha*. The writing is clear and immediate, and the ideas are so applicable to the real daily issues of leading. More than a book, this program offers Do Nows, interactive activities, journal exercises, self-assessments, and mini-assignments that will make concepts come alive and help you to integrate all the valuable ideas into your real life. Halfway through the book I had already changed two habits! A great guide for being the best leader you can be in work, with family, with friends, and in life. —Jesse Sage Noonan, EdD, Chief Academic Officer for the Youth Policy Institute

This is as much a book about who the "New Alphas" are as it is a guide-book for how to embody this approach to leadership. Harlan weaves definitions, descriptions, and stories together to help you understand "New Alpha" distinctions, and then helps you discover where you are in the spectrum. She also provides you with incredibly diverse, real-life, and creative strategies for developing your self-assessed areas for growth on each of *The New Alpha* leadership competencies. I particularly like her ideas for maintaining your "circle of support" and practicing gratitude, as they apply specifically to my life. Expect these and other life-altering nuggets as you read and work your way through the program.

—ANDY PETRANEK, coach, entrepreneur, founder,
and co-CEO Whole Life Challenge

From real-life examples to templates and accountability trackers, *The New Alpha* delivers: This is not just a book but a guide to living a life of meaning and impact. Harlan's direct and practical approach is sprinkled with humility, reflection, and humor. She makes New Alpha leadership approachable and attainable for all.

—AHNNA SMITH, government and nonprofit executive

Compelling, inspirational, and motivational! *The New Alpha* provides data, stories, and techniques to tap into your strengths and create a lifelong plan for your personal growth and leadership development. A must-read for all who strive to be the best they can be!

—KIM MEREDITH, executive director,
Stanford Center on Philanthropy and Civil Society

Redefining success requires a practical framework, built on data-driven insights and a holistic view of your life. Harlan delivers an enduring new leadership model for the Future of Work.

—SALLY THORNTON, CEO and founder of Forshay and TEDx speaker

The New Alpha forges a path for anyone aspiring to a vision of success that goes beyond the next rung of the ladder in your industry. Danielle Harlan paints a picture of leadership grounded in impact, fulfillment, and self-actualization—a breath of fresh air in the business literature. It's rare that a book so deftly provides actionable insights while not promising superficial quick fixes. There's no way you'll come away from this book without being a more focused, purposeful, authentic, and self-possessed leader.

—ROB STRAIN, partner at Transcend Education

Danielle Harlan is cheering you on to be the best leader you can be. In this book she guides you with a steady hand, a clear mind, and a moral compass.

—HEATHER KIRKPATRICK, PhD, president and CEO of Aspire University and former Chief People Office for Aspire Public Schools

Want to take your life and leadership to the next level—but not sure where to begin? A far cry from the typical "leadership" book, *The New Alpha* is filled with inspiring stories and actionable advice that will help you to define your purpose, formulate a plan, and maximize your impact.

—ANNE LOEHR, author of *A Manager's Guide to Coaching* and *Managing the Unmanageable*, named the "Generational Guru" by *The Washington Post*

At last, a leadership book that recognizes that for one to be outstanding in his or her craft, balance and one's unique voice sets the foundation. For all, the return on time investment by reading *The New Alpha* will be exponential.

—CATHERINE M. CASSERLY, PhD, Catalyst for Openness, Leadership, and Innovation in Education; former CEO of Creative Commons; and Aspen Institute Fellow

THE NEW ALPHA

THE NEW ALPHA

Join the Rising Movement of Influencers and Changemakers Who Are Redefining Leadership

DANIELLE HARLAN, PhD

NEW YORK   CHICAGO   SAN FRANCISCO   ATHENS
LONDON   MADRID   MEXICO CITY   MILAN
NEW DELHI   SINGAPORE   SYDNEY   TORONTO

1 2 3 4 5 6 7 8 9   QFR   21 20 19 18 17 16

ISBN   978-1-259-64191-6
MHID   1-259-64191-0

e-ISBN 978-1-259-64192-3
e-MHID   1-259-64192-9

Design by Mauna Eichner and Lee Fukui

McGraw-Hill Education books are available at special quantity discounts to use as premiums and sales promotions or for use in corporate training programs. To contact a representative, please visit the Contact Us pages at www.mhprofessional.com.

To the New Alphas everywhere (including you, dear reader):
I'm honored and humbled to be your scribe.

Our lives are not our own. We are bound to others,
past and present, and by each crime and every kindness,
we birth our future.
—DAVID MITCHELL, British author

A portion of the author's royalties will be donated to organizations
that support universal human rights.

Contents

PART I
PERSONAL EXCELLENCE

PART II
PERSONAL LEADERSHIP

PART III
TEAM AND ORGANIZATIONAL
LEADERSHIP

Author's Note

The stories shared in this book come from real people whom I've known and worked with. In most cases, I've used their real names (denoted by a first and last name). However, in some cases, to protect their anonymity, I've changed the name of the person and used only a first name. In these situations, I've also changed any identifying information and details.

Welcome to the New Alpha Movement

*Greater than the tread of mighty armies
is an idea whose time has come.*
—Victor Hugo, French poet, novelist, and dramatist

JAMILA AND JARROD: A TALE OF TWO ALPHAS

*A great person attracts great people and
knows how to hold them together.*
—Johann Wolfgang von Goethe,
German writer and statesperson

Have you ever met one of those incredibly awesome and impressive people whom you also genuinely enjoy being around and who makes you feel excited and inspired about whatever they're working on? You know the type—they tend to be high achieving but also totally healthy and balanced, ethical, and in possession of a seemingly endless supply of motivation and energy. Whether they're teachers, supervisors, team leaders, or even colleagues or classmates, these people are a pleasure to be around, and interacting with them makes you feel empowered and ready to take on the world. I don't know why, maybe because I was trained as a social scientist, but whenever I meet these people, rare unicorns that they are, I want to study them like crazy and understand their magic.

I remember my first in-depth encounter with one of these exceptional human beings. Her name was Jamila Hall, and she was the student instructor for my first-semester introductory honors course in college. It's hard to put my finger on exactly what made her so distinctive. True, she was incredibly successful academically—she had been awarded a full scholarship to college, she had graduated *summa cum laude*, she had received a fellowship to attend Columbia Law School, and she had won a ton of awards. But there was something more that made her special, something beyond the honors and accolades.

When you were in her course, you felt inspired, as if she were driven by something deeper than the desire to be "successful." She talked openly about problems in the world, such as war, racism, poverty, and poor leadership, and she spoke earnestly about her belief that each of us had something to contribute.

Perhaps even more impressive was that Jamila seemed to genuinely enjoy life and appreciate experiences beyond her schoolwork and student leadership activities—like spending time with her family and friends, traveling the world, and learning new things. After years of feeling caught in the hamster wheel of social pressure and expectations around achievement, it was truly refreshing to meet someone who openly valued regular exercise and time with her boyfriend (now her spouse) as much as anything else. In fact, it often seemed that these aspects of her life both fueled her motivation and determination to tackle big goals and were integral to her definition of success.

Through my relationship with Jamila, I began to redefine success and to see leadership as something more than the next logical step in my accomplishment-driven life. I realized that, at its best, *leadership is about becoming the best version of yourself in order to maximize your positive impact on the world. It's about developing into someone whom people genuinely respect and admire and want to work with—and using that power and influence to be a force for good in the world.*

Obviously, not every leader is like this though. I remember another instance when I worked for a supervisor named "Jarrod." Jarrod was also an incredibly accomplished and award-winning professional with a number of degrees from Ivy League schools and plenty of executive-level experience at several well-known organizations. Unfortunately, he was also a total nightmare to work with.

Despite the fact that he talked a good game around values-driven leadership and acting ethically and respectfully in the workplace, he regularly took credit for my work and aggressively chastised me for unintentional and minor mistakes. He once even chewed me out for answering a question that his assistant happened to ask me. It wasn't my answer that he didn't like. It was that *I* had the audacity to answer *his* assistant's question when he felt that only he should be allowed to do that.

Perhaps most frustrating was that Jarrod also frequently overruled my decisions and then openly blamed me for the subsequent unsuccessful outcomes. Eventually, when Jarrod began gossiping to me about other employees and managers, it finally hit me that the empathetic and virtuous persona that he strived to cultivate publicly was little more than a carefully developed façade to conceal the fact that he did whatever was necessary to get what he wanted from others or to make himself look like a hero in difficult situations.

My experience working with Jarrod was the polar opposite of my experience with Jamila. With Jarrod, I felt unmotivated, stressed out, and unhappy, and after a number of efforts to remedy the situation, I—like many of the people who worked for him—eventually moved on to a different role with a better supervisor.

In retrospect, despite my challenges with Jarrod, I'm grateful for having had the experience to work with such a self-serving and incompetent leader. (It's always easy to say that after the fact!) Having interacted and worked with people like Jamila and Jarrod, as well as countless others, many of whom fell somewhere in between their two extremes, I eventually recognized a basic truth about leadership: *regardless of their official title or position, people who strive for excellence in all areas of their lives and who can bring big ideas to life—especially those rooted in a purpose greater than themselves—are often the best and most inspiring leaders.* To them, success and power are incidental—merely the positive side effects of endeavoring toward more noble pursuits. I call these people the New Alphas, and you and I are fortunate enough to be alive at a time when an increasing number of people are embracing this new and better approach to leadership.

WHO ARE THE NEW ALPHAS?

I believe that each of us comes from the
creator trailing wisps of glory.
—MAYA ANGELOU,
American author, poet, and civil rights activist

So what does it mean to be an Alpha anyway? In astronomy, the brightest star in a constellation is typically called the *alpha*. Likewise in the animal kingdom, the *alpha* is the most dominant animal in the group. And so it goes in human affairs that we generally think of influential and powerful people as *alphas*. Let's be honest, though—most of the time we don't like these people, and when we think of them, we don't typically think of someone like Jamila. Instead, we think of a person who is similar to Jarrod—and herein lies the problem with the traditional Alpha model.

Many of us have an aversion to the Alpha label because we are inundated with messages telling us that if we want to be powerful—that is, if we want to get things done and influence others—then we must lie, cheat, and take other people down along the way. For instance, let's look at the events from a single random week in 2015. A major news reporter was caught lying about his experiences in the field, the president of a country was being investigated for allegedly putting out a hit on an "unfriendly" prosecutor, and a state governor resigned amid allegations that he violated conflict of interest rules by awarding contracts to his romantic partner. I'm sure you can think of similar examples from the recent news or even your own life. The point is that this pattern of behavior has become so prevalent that it's hard to imagine people being successful or powerful without also being willing to sell their soul.

And yet, if you think back to your own experiences, you can probably also remember at least one leader you have known who seemed to break the mold—someone who was high achieving and influential while also working to be an exemplary and balanced human being. When we talk about New Alphas, these are the people we're talking about. What's more, their approach to leadership is a radical shift away from the traditional Alpha model that we're used to, and it is rooted in *three core beliefs*:

1. Each of us possesses the innate potential to make a unique and meaningful impact in the world. When we recognize and harness this potential, we naturally inspire and motivate others, increase our influence, and enhance our ability to ignite positive change in our lives, our organizations, and the world.

2. By working to become the best version of ourselves, we develop the foundational competencies that are necessary to effectively lead others.

3. Being a *successful* leader is about more than what we achieve or accomplish. It's also about enjoying life and having a positive impact

on others and the world around us. It is these latter aspects of success that give us the motivation and stamina to productively persist through difficult challenges—and that give our lives meaning and purpose in the long run.

Driven by these core beliefs, New Alpha leaders focus on developing their competencies across three critical domains: *personal excellence, personal leadership*, and *team and organizational leadership*.

While the New Alphas come from a variety of organizations, fields, and roles, they are unified in their unwavering belief that the status quo isn't working and that there is a better way to lead. The remainder of this book provides an overview of the New Alpha leadership philosophy that I've learned by working with and studying this growing movement of influencers and changemakers over the course of my professional career as a leader, a scholar, and a coach. It also includes the tools, resources, and exercises that will help you to grow and develop into a New Alpha leader.

HOW THIS BOOK IS DIFFERENT

More than a book, *The New Alpha* is a holistic and interactive leadership and personal development program that is designed to help you optimize your human potential while also increasing your competency as a leader. The New Alpha program is distinctive from other leadership books in several important ways:

- **It's a developmental framework—not simply another book filled with lists of advice and life hacks.** Rather than reading though a lot of great information and then feeling overwhelmed and not sure where to start, you'll work through the various stages of the program, track your progress, and make changes along the way. Each step builds on what's come before, and you're free to work through it at your own pace.

- **It's data driven.** Many leadership and personal development programs fail because they don't require you to track your progress and make strategic changes as you learn what works and what doesn't. The New Alpha program is different in that tracking progress and making changes are key aspects of the program, and these routines are built in from the start.

- **It's customizable.** While this program is designed to give you the information and resources that will support your growth and development as a New Alpha leader, each part is also structured to be flexible so that you can modify it or adapt it to best meet your needs.

- **It's thorough.** The New Alpha program digs deeply into the *what*, *why*, and *how* of leadership and personal development. More than providing a list of goals to work toward or actions to take, we'll talk about how you can implement the ideas from this book. We'll also include step-by-step instructions, examples, and ideas and recommendations from other New Alphas.

- **We follow the No B^!!$#*t Rule.** The New Alpha program is based not only on the experiences of many individuals in this growing movement of leaders but also on the best of what we know from science and philosophy. It's not a quick fix, and it's going to be challenging. However, it's also a highly effective and practical approach to exceptional leadership for those of us who are willing to put in the required hard work and commitment.

- **It's a community.** While *The New Alpha* is a leadership and personal development program, we are also a growing movement of people striving to forge a new and better path to power and success, and we couldn't be more excited to invite you to join us on this ambitious, adventurous, and challenging journey!

HOW THIS BOOK IS ORGANIZED

This book is organized in three parts. Part I, "Personal Excellence," focuses on helping you to develop the foundational habits that you'll need to be a happy, healthy, high-achieving, and inspiring human being. In this part, we'll cover character and ethics, positive and productive relationships with others, health and wellness, and developing a mindset for success. You'll also begin the process of setting personal goals, tracking your progress, and adjusting your course as necessary. This part wraps up with an overview of the psychological and organizational strategies and tactics that will support you on your journey—especially when your energy or motivation wanes (which, by the way, happens to everyone at one point or another).

In Part II, "Personal Leadership," you'll identify your *Personal Leadership Identity*—that is, the unique combination of gifts and talents that you bring to the world. You'll also reflect on how this affects your approach to leadership. Finally, you'll learn about and begin to apply a three-phase process, Vision-Plan-Execute (VPE), in order to identify your long-term personal vision and bring it to life.

In Part III, "Team and Organizational Leadership," you'll build on what you learned in Parts I and II and work to develop additional competencies that will help you to effectively lead and manage others in a variety of challenging contexts and situations.

A word of fair warning: this is not the kind of book that you sit down and read in a single sitting (at least not if you want to be able to apply what you're reading about). As you work through each of the chapters, you'll frequently pause to take self-assessments and engage in activities and exercises that will help you to internalize and apply what you're learning. You'll also track your progress and make improvements as you go.

Space is provided in the book to do each of the activities and exercises that are included. However, if you prefer not to write in this book, I recommend keeping a notebook, journal, or word processing document available so that you have ample space to do the activities (and so that you can refer back to your responses to these activities, as necessary in the future). Also, be sure to keep your calendar or planner handy so that you can note any future to-dos or follow-ups that you identify along the way. If it's helpful, you might form a small group of people to work through the content together, share ideas, and provide mutual encouragement.

If you'd like to learn more about the topics covered in this book, we've developed *The New Alpha Resource Guide* to accompany the book. You can download this resource guide for free at www.LeadershipAndHumanPotential.com/Resources. In the spirit of building a movement, please feel free to share this resource guide with anyone else who might benefit from it.

Finally, while the material in this book is based on the best that we know from science and philosophy, as well as ideas and recommendations from hundreds of people whom I've observed and interviewed over the years, you should feel free to adjust and tweak it to make it your own.

In fact, it's entirely possible that your personal spin on this material will be greater than anything the rest of us could have imagined, so don't let the prescriptive nature of this program (or my enthusiasm for a particular way of doing something!) dissuade you from what you think will work best. This is your life and your journey—*you* are the one in charge. I'm just here to support you along the way.

OUR CONTRACT

As a coach, I ask my clients to sign contracts committing to our work together. (I sign one as well.) This contract makes our shared expectations and obligations explicit, and, in my experience, it also helps people take the step of proactively committing themselves to the program, which increases their motivation to keep at it—even when it becomes challenging to do so. With this in mind, take a moment to review and sign the following contract, and then snap a picture of it, print it or write it out by hand, and post it in a place where you can see it every day. For additional support and motivation, you can subscribe to our free newsletter (www.LeadershipAndHumanPotential.com/Newsletter) and join the conversation on social media.

Commitment to the New Alpha Leadership Program

I, _____, hereby commit to working through the New Alpha leadership program in its entirety, meaning that I will complete all of the reading and learning activities, including tracking, and follow-up, however long it may take. I understand that the process of learning and applying the New Alpha leadership principles will be intensive and challenging, and it may radically change my life—and I commit to being patient and supportive of myself during this process.

On behalf of all of us, welcome to the New Alpha movement!

THE NEW ALPHA

PART I

PERSONAL EXCELLENCE

This part of the New Alpha program is designed to help you develop the foundational habits that you'll need to successfully lead others, realize your personal vision, and live a fulfilling and impactful life. In this part of the program, you'll also gain experience with setting goals, tracking progress, and using data about your performance to make improvements.

Chapters 1 through 4 in this part are strategically sequenced to help you find a healthy balance between developing yourself and showing care and concern for others:

- Chapter 1, "Demonstrate Character and Ethics," outlines five *moral and ethical habits* that will help you be the best human being you can be.

- Chapter 2, "Build Positive and Productive Relationships with Others," will help you develop the *interpersonal habits* that will support healthy and fulfilling relationships with the people in your life.

- Chapter 3, "Prioritize Your Health and Wellness," covers five research-based *health habits* that will help you sustain high performance *and* well-being in your life and work.

- Chapter 4, "Develop a Mindset for Success," focuses on establishing the *mental habits* that will support your long-term success.

Each of these chapters is divided into sections that cover the foundational habits that will support your long-term success. Each section, in turn, includes a subsection called "How to Make It Happen" that provides additional ideas, resources, and exercises to help you incorporate the habit into your everyday life. The "Wrap-Up and Tracking Progress" section will explain how to track your progress and make changes as you go.

Chapter 5, "Psychological and Organizational Strategies to Help You Achieve Your Goals," is designed to help you work through any aspects of the previous chapters that you find particularly challenging *and* to arm you with strategies that will support your success in Part II, "Personal Leadership," and Part III, "Team and Organizational Leadership."

Sound good? Okay, let's jump in!

Demonstrate Character and Ethics

*Good actions give strength to ourselves and
inspire good actions in others.*
—Plato, classical Greek philosopher

On the evening of Thursday, April 12, 2012, Cory Booker (then mayor of Newark, now Senator Cory Booker) was returning home from a media event when he heard screaming from a nearby neighbor's house. The house was on fire, and at least one person was still trapped in an upstairs bedroom. Without thinking, Cory jumped into action. His security team members, who were assigned to protect him, initially tried to prevent him from entering the burning building, but they ultimately relented when he ordered them to let him go. Cory ran into the building, found the trapped person, and, with the help of his team, carried her out of the house, before finally collapsing in a fit of coughing on the front lawn. (He was later treated at the hospital for smoke inhalation and second-degree burns.)

When I mentioned this event to a friend of mine who knows Cory, he said that he had emailed Cory to congratulate him on the good deed and received the most sincere and self-effacing response back, something to the effect of, "Thanks, but I was actually terrified!" Look, I'm not saying that Cory Booker is a saint, but his virtuous actions and responses in this scenario paint a powerfully different image of leadership than we're used to, which is exciting and hopeful.

Decisions like the one Cory made to risk his own well-being in order to help someone else, while also not getting caught up in his own hype, remind us that there's more to life and leadership than what we gain personally. While traditional Alpha leaders tend to focus on personal success and optimizing bottom-line goals, like profits and revenues, New Alpha leaders, *above all else* balance their individual and organizational needs with concern for their community and the world around them.

In particular, there are *five essential habits relating to character virtues and ethical principles* that we New Alphas try our best to develop, and it's our consistent practice of these habits that builds our strength and influence over time. These five habits are:

- Show kindness and generosity

- Be courageous and act with integrity

- Cultivate humility

- Be industrious

- Practice good citizenship and stewardship

SELF-ASSESSMENT

Rank yourself (1 = greatest area for growth, 5 = greatest area of strength) on each of the following aspects of character and ethics. You may use each number (1 to 5) only once:

1. ___I feel concern for others' happiness and well-being. I'm friendly and treat others fairly and respectfully, and I regularly share my resources with others.

2. ___I am honest and principled. I do what is right even in the face of strong pressure and/or the threat of personal harm or injury. I am trustworthy and not gossipy.

3. ___I am modest and able to recognize my limitations. I keep success in perspective.

4. ___I am hardworking and give my best effort to everything that I do. I take personal responsibility for the outcomes of the projects that I'm involved in.

5. ___I am a conscientious, responsible, and contributing member of the community, and, when necessary, I can put the needs of the group ahead of my own needs or desires.

In the space below, take note of how you rated yourself across these five items. This will help you to prioritize the sections of this chapter that you should focus on first.

My Responses

1. ___ Topic: Show kindness and generosity

2. ___ Topic: Be courageous and act with integrity

3. ___ Topic: Cultivate humility

4. ___ Topic: Be industrious

5. ___Topic: Practice good citizenship and stewardship

SHOW KINDNESS AND GENEROSITY

*Hello, babies. Welcome to Earth. It's hot in the summer and
cold in the winter. It's round and wet and crowded.
At the outside, babies, you've got about a hundred years here.
There's only one rule that I know of, babies—God damn it,
you've got to be kind.*
—KURT VONNEGUT, American author

Showing kindness and generosity means demonstrating *genuine* concern for others' happiness and well-being, being friendly, and giving more to others than is necessary or expected. More than just being nice to people or helping them because we think we *should* act this way or because we *need something from them*, this habit is all about embracing our inner altruistic spirit and letting this aspect of our personality really shine in a sincere and other-centered way. When we act in accordance with this aspect of character and ethics, we not only strengthen our interpersonal relationships and make others feel good but we also increase the amount of joy that we feel on a daily basis, so it's a total win-win-win situation.

My graduate school advisor and dissertation chair, David Brady, professor of political science and leadership values at Stanford University, exemplifies kindness and generosity. I remember everyone talking about him during our graduate student Admit Weekend at Stanford, and I (having never met him) couldn't figure out why on earth he was so popular. When I finally encountered him during my first month as a graduate student, I immediately understood why everyone loved him. Aside from being wicked smart and completely hilarious (he once told me he was surprised that the entire Hoover Institute, a somewhat conservative-leaning think tank, didn't collapse when I, an avowed liberal, entered), his concern for others was evident from the get-go. Whether he's buying lunch for a graduate seminar or connecting students with prominent researchers in their field of interest, he's always considering the needs of others and thinking about what resources he can bring to bear in order to advance their success. What I appreciate most about David is that, no matter what your background or experiences (in my case: being a liberal), he's always eager to talk with people, challenge his own views, and help you in whatever way he can.

How to Make It Happen

DO NOW →→→→→→→→→→

Implement one item from the list below each day for the next five days. When you are finished, use this space to jot down a few quick notes about your experience—what went well, what challenges came up (if any), what surprises occurred, and what else you would like to try from this list or from your own list.

- When emailing your colleagues, before you write what you want or need from them, remember to recognize and appreciate them as human beings by wishing them well. (Try this: "Dear X, First off, I hope you're having a great start of your week.")

- Buy the person behind you a cup of coffee the next time you're at your favorite local coffee shop.

- Volunteer to serve food at your local food bank once a month (or once a week . . . or more!). Visit www.onebrick.org or www.volunteermatch .org for more information on volunteer options in your area.

- Write a thank-you card to a colleague who helped you on a big project.

- Send flowers to your grandmother.

- Leave a $10 tip on a $20 meal—I can say from personal experience that serving is one of the most difficult jobs out there, and leaving a generous tip will definitely make someone's day.

- Send a thank-you card or email to your favorite childhood teacher.

- Ask someone who's serving you (at a restaurant, a coffee shop, the post office) how she's doing today.

- Listen patiently, and without interrupting, to someone who needs to vent.

- Compliment someone at work for a job well done.

- Sit with someone at lunch who's new to your workplace or group.

- Find a way to support a cause that you believe in—by giving time and/ or money.

- Hold the door for someone.

- Tell the person or people who raised you that you love them.

- Look for opportunities to help people without being asked.

- Pick a non-December holiday and send out cards to everyone you care about. I have a friend, Katharine Schweighardt, who does this for Valentine's Day, and it always makes me smile!

My notes on the kindness and generosity experiment:

BE COURAGEOUS AND ACT WITH INTEGRITY

The time is always right to do what is right.
—MARTIN LUTHER KING, JR.,
American Baptist minister, activist,
humanitarian, and leader in the
African-American civil rights movement

Being courageous and acting with integrity means being honest and principled—and doing what's right, even in the face of strong pressure and/or the threat of harm to your person, your job, or something else. It also means being trustworthy and not gossipy. If you're Cory Booker, being courageous and acting with integrity may mean running into a burning building to save someone, but this habit can also be demonstrated in other ways, in everything from following through on your commitments to people to graciously pointing out when a certain policy or decision may unfairly disadvantage a particular person or group. It also means apologizing immediately and sincerely when you realize that you've made a mistake, even if you are worried about how this will make you look to others.

How to Make It Happen
In my experience, it's very easy to judge others for their failures in courage and integrity, but when you're the one in the hot seat, it can be hard to think quickly and clearly about how to best handle a difficult situation, particularly like the ones involving ethical "gray areas." In these cases, Professor Philip Zimbardo (organizer of the famous Stanford Prison Experiment) gives five pieces of advice on how to foster a "hero" mindset:

1. **Proactively look for opportunities in which you can be a good person—especially instances when this is hard to do.** Where do you see suffering or something happening that just doesn't jibe with your internal moral compass?

2. **Learn to be okay with causing interpersonal conflict and controversy.** While knowing how to play the peacemaker role can be important, knowing when to stand up for what's right can be equally,

if not more, valuable. If you struggle with finding the right way to do this, try rehearsing what you'll say or do beforehand.

3. **Take a long view of the situation—what might happen if you don't act?** It's sometimes tempting to lay low and keep your mouth shut when something controversial comes up, but I've found that it's more difficult for me to do this when I think about what bad might come of my avoiding the situation or just remaining "neutral."

4. **Don't try to sugarcoat a bad situation by spinning it in your head as if it's somehow good or as if it will ultimately lead to good and desirable results.** See things for what they are, and do what is right.

5. **Be okay with upsetting or angering people, especially those in positions of authority.** Trust that you'll be validated—by others, or by the universe—in the long run. Honestly, I'm convinced that the biggest barrier to exceptional leadership for my generation is our desire to maintain harmony and not upset people. Sure, this can be a powerful skill in certain situations, but not when it allows bad behavior to go unchecked. As someone with experience in acting both courageously *and* cowardly in various difficult situations, I can honestly say that the burden of being not liked by others is far easier to deal with than the burden of knowing that you are not the kind of person you want to be. One is personally and professionally difficult; the other is spiritually and existentially difficult.[1]

If all else fails, and you find yourself in a situation in which you're pretty sure you need to speak up but you aren't certain about the best way to do this, you can always try the "I'm confused . . ." model. This idea, suggested to me by a former professor, basically entails not rushing to make a judgment about what's right or wrong about a decision or behavior but merely asking open-ended and probing questions and having the person in charge explain her rationale.

Originally, the feminist inside of me didn't like this model because I felt like it entailed "playing dumb," but over time, I realized it's really just about suspending judgment and being curious in a nonthreatening way. It's also a surprisingly effective method that you can use if you're one of the people in the room with the least amount of power or influence.

For example, let's say I'm a new teacher in a cash-strapped school district, and one of my students, because of her disability, is legally required to have a one-on-one instructional aide. However, the district can't afford it and thus isn't providing this service to the student (a decision which is, by the way, illegal). In this situation, I can either take the cowardly way out and not stand up for my student and what she's entitled to, or I can push the district administrators to provide the aide. But if I'm too pushy, they might get annoyed with me, and they might even find a reason to get rid of me (and remember, I'm new at this job, and I have zero tenure, so I'm trying hard to not get fired or irritate anyone).

So, here's where I might say to a district official, "Hmm, I totally hear what you're saying, and it sounds like this is an expensive service for us to provide, but I'm confused: I thought this child was legally entitled to the one-on-one aide, and aren't we out of compliance if we don't provide this?" Then I shut my mouth and wait for her to respond. We may have a little bit of back and forth before the issue is resolved, but by communicating in a nonthreatening way, letting this person know that I understand where she's coming from, and by expressing my concern that "we" (not "she") might be out of compliance, I use my *emotional intelligence* (see Chapter 2, "Build Positive and Productive Relationships with Others") to help her see that we need to provide this service.

So the next thing that people usually ask me is, "Well, what if the district official still refuses to provide the service that this student needs?" There are lots of options here: I could covertly tip off the parents and refer them to an organization that would help them push for this service, or I could seek advice from a trusted mentor, like the principal or another more experienced teacher. Personally, I prefer the persistent, but still cooperative and nonthreatening route because it tends to be highly effective and helps to preserve the working relationship (which is usually very helpful in the long run). But if I found myself in a situation in which the district was absolutely unwilling to budge and the child was being denied a service to which she or he was legally entitled, I would think long and hard about who I am as a person and whether I'd rather have a job that forced me to act against my values, and the law, or risk being fired for what I believed in. And for the record, risking your livelihood when you have no backup plan or money is not an easy thing to do (especially when you have bills to pay), but it's a decision that almost always goes better if you've thought about it in advance and you are clear on what matters most to you.

CULTIVATE HUMILITY

*Avoid putting yourself before others and you can
become a leader among [others].*
—LAO TZU, ancient Chinese philosopher and writer

Cultivating humility means being modest and recognizing your potential limitations. It also means remembering to keep success in perspective and not getting caught up in our own awesomeness. For instance, I once had a colleague who was just out of college, and by day three of his first full-time job, he was already talking about being bored and wanting a promotion. While this probably would have come across as arrogant even if he had already risen to rock star status in his new role, the fact that he wasn't even able to perform the basic duties for his current job made him look both arrogant *and* incompetent—a powerfully bad combination.

Since that time, he's bounced around from job to job with basically the same complaint about all of them: they're just not recognizing how great he is. Don't get me wrong, we live in a time when it makes sense to be open to the possibility of taking on new and exciting challenges. But if you find yourself changing jobs every 6 to 12 months and/or repeatedly hearing the same critical feedback from your colleagues and supervisors, it *may* be a sign that the issue is internal rather than external.

How to Make It Happen
Be proactive about seeking feedback. Not surprisingly, the highest-performing leaders I know are the ones who constantly seek feedback—from their supervisors, colleagues, and staff members. They are curious about both what they do well *and* how they can continue to grow and improve. More than just being super self-aware and high performing, these people also come across as totally confident and secure in their abilities.

My guess is that they sometimes get feedback that's hard to hear, but it's better to hear it earlier—and from people you know and trust—than later, when everyone else knows and the issues have affected your credibility. Also, remember to thank people for the gift of feedback. Keep in mind that no matter how painful it feels to receive critical feedback, the givers wouldn't share it with you unless they believed that you were capable of doing more and being better.

DO NOW

Make a note to ask your supervisor to give you feedback about one thing that you are doing well in your current role and one way that you could improve. Ask her or him about this during your next check-in. Capture your notes and reflections from this conversation in the space below.

What I do well:

What I could improve upon:

Recognize your limitations, and be open to continuously learning and improving. No one is perfect, and we all have our flaws and limitations, but New Alpha leaders are ruthlessly honest with themselves about their areas for growth, and they take *strategic action* to improve in these areas—by finding a coach, creating an improvement plan, or taking a course or program designed to target the areas that they want to further develop.

DO NOW

What is one thing that you could improve about yourself in order to increase your odds of personal or professional success? Identify three to four actions that you can take to make this change:

One thing that I could improve about myself:

Three to four actions that I could take to make this change:

→ → → → → → → → → → → →

Be thoughtful about how and when you celebrate your successes. If you and I know each other personally, chances are good that I've encouraged you to create a celebration board (which we will discuss in the "Embrace Failure and Continuous Improvement" section in Chapter 4, "Develop a Mindset for Success"). I love celebrating wins, and I have learned that taking the time to celebrate is a critical component of staying positive, energetic, and motivated while working toward long-term goals.

That said, there's a right way to celebrate and a wrong way to celebrate, and if you find yourself in a situation in which your celebrations are starting to outweigh your actual accomplishments or if your celebrations are over the top in a way that's obnoxious, then you're putting your credibility and relatability at risk—two situations that are likely to hinder your ability to influence and motivate people in the long run. Being both humble and owning your success is a careful (but important!) balance that can look different for different people—your goal is to experiment and find what works best for you.

BE INDUSTRIOUS

Nothing ever comes to one, that is worth having,
except as a result of hard work.
—Booker T. Washington, American educator, author,
orator, and advisor to presidents of the United States

Being industrious means feeling a high degree of personal responsibility for getting things done, and it means working hard and smart—including and especially when you're tired and progress seems impossible. A good example would be working relentlessly to complete an important group project with a tight deadline, rather than sitting back and letting your teammates shoulder the burden.

As a leader and manager, being industrious means that you should never entirely abandon your team to "go at it alone" on a big project. Sure, you want to avoid micromanaging people who are otherwise performing well, but even if your sole responsibility is to simply check in with your people and clear obstacles, be sure to actually do this!

Being industrious doesn't mean that you should be a workaholic, but it does mean that you should *do the right work (high leverage), at the right time (high priority), in the right way (efficiently)*. Working this way also allows you to feel more comfortable *truly disconnecting* when you're not working.

How to Make It Happen

Chapter 5, "Psychological and Organizational Strategies to Help You Achieve Your Goals," lists a variety of ideas and advice that will help you to finish what you start. However, if the idea of working relentlessly seems a little daunting or overwhelming, here are three strategies that will help you embody this aspect of character and ethics:

1. Choose projects that motivate you. If you feel naturally motivated to do one type of work over another, try to seek out and take on tasks and projects that allow you to capitalize on this internal motivation. For instance, if you ask me to develop a strategic plan or develop a budget, I will almost always work harder on (and be more excited about) the strategic planning work. This doesn't mean that I can't or don't do budget work (I love math!), but where possible I try to delegate these types of tasks to people who are more naturally motivated to do it.

DO NOW →→→→→→→→→→

In the chart in Figure 1.1, identify three tasks or projects that you've completed in the past year that you enjoyed doing (not just accomplishing but actually doing). These do not necessarily have to be work related. For each one, describe why you enjoyed doing it. What personal or professional projects or tasks can you take on in the near future that will allow you to leverage this same internal motivation?

Task or Project That I Enjoyed Doing	Why I Enjoyed Doing it	Similar Tasks or Projects That I Can Take on in the Future

Figure 1.1 Identify Three Tasks or Projects You Have Completed in the Past Year That You Enjoyed Doing

→→→→→→→→→→→

2. Manage your energy. If you are tired or just not taking care of your body properly, you're going to have a difficult time mustering the energy necessary to do hard (intellectual or physical) work. It's also likely to affect your mindset and ability to build positive and productive relationships with others. Unless something is truly urgent and mission critical, give yourself permission to stop working at a reasonable hour, get some rest, and take care of your other (non-work-related) needs. (See Chapter 3, "Prioritize Your Health and Wellness," for additional ideas and advice about how to make this happen.)

3. Work smart. No matter who you are, or what you do, we've all had the experience of feeling overwhelmed with too much to do and not enough time in which to do it. New Alpha leaders don't just work hard. They work smart: by prioritizing urgent and important work over nonurgent and unimportant work[2] and by creating efficiencies in their life and work (for example, combining meetings, combining exercise with social events, or preplanning their weekly meals). They're also not afraid to go back and drop activities or responsibilities that don't support their big-picture goals.

DO NOW

What are your top (no more than three!) personal and/or professional priorities right now? Given these priorities, are you allocating your time appropriately? If not, what changes do you need to make?

My top (no more than three) priorities:

Changes that I can make to better focus on these areas of my life and work:

PRACTICE GOOD CITIZENSHIP AND STEWARDSHIP

The greatest danger to our future is apathy.
—Jane Goodall,
British primatologist,
ethologist, anthropologist, and
UN Messenger of Peace

Practicing good citizenship and stewardship means being a conscientious, responsible, and contributing member of the community and—in some cases—putting the needs of the group ahead of your own. Examples of this include voting and being politically engaged (even if you're not a member of a political party), keeping up on current events, being environmentally friendly, and supporting the work and development of your community.

Being a good citizen and steward takes time and energy, but it's also the price we each must pay if we want our groups and society to survive and flourish. Think about it this way: have you ever worked in a place with a fantastic organizational culture, happy employees, and high productivity, but where people, or leaders especially, refused to do their fair share of the "community" work, like cleaning up after themselves, planning events, or participating in "mandatory" trainings and workshops? I didn't think so.

To simplify a lot of complex political and economic theory: *each of us has to do our part to contribute to, and care for, the community unless we want you-know-what to hit the fan.*

How to Make It Happen

Be politically engaged. Let's face it: our current political climate leaves something to be desired. With all of the mud-slinging, illegal and unethical behavior, and propaganda going on around us, it can be painful and frustrating to participate in our political system. But make no mistake, whether we like them or not, the people whom we elect to office are making decisions that affect our lives in ways big and small, and by disengaging from the political world, we are simply allowing them to perpetuate bad policies and unjust laws. I'm not saying you have to run for office, but at the very least, you should do the necessary research and vote.

DO NOW →→ → → → → → → →

- If you are not already registered to vote in your municipality, state, or country, sign up now! (Google "register to vote" for instructions on how to do this.)

- If you haven't yet made up your mind on one or more controversial issues, the website www.procon.org does a nice job of laying out the arguments for and against a variety of contemporary issues. (Note that this site is mainly United States focused, but it covers topics that are relevant to the broader international community as well.)

→→ → → → → → → → →

Know what's going on in the world. One of the most frightening comments that I frequently hear from peers is that they no longer read (or watch, or follow, or whatever) the news. Don't get me wrong—I get that we live in a time when information is streaming at us full time from every angle, and stemming the information overflow can be a good thing. But completely disregarding what's going on in the world is, frankly, selfish and promotes the kind of small-minded ignorance that is becoming a real headache in our modern world.

With this in mind (and for the love of all that is good and decent), try to find at least one reasonably unbiased source of daily news (that is, not a blog—though blogs can be interesting and useful secondary references). See *The New Alpha Resource Guide* for a list of some of my favorite options.

Subscribing to a *real* news source doesn't mean that you can't also read other articles or watch the news (or the fake news on *The Daily Show*). However, make sure that you're getting at least a few minutes of *actual* news each day, so that you're familiar with the events of the day and can have an opinion on issues that affect your life, your community, and the things that matter to you.

DO NOW ⟶ ⟶ ⟶ ⟶ ⟶ ⟶ ⟶ ⟶ ⟶ ⟶

Commit to accessing at least one (relatively unbiased) news source each day. If you plan to watch on your television or computer (or stream from an app), then set a calendar reminder *right now* to remind yourself. If you prefer to subscribe to a daily news update via email, sign up *right now*. Your well-informed and thoughtful future self will thank you.

⟶ ⟶ ⟶ ⟶ ⟶ ⟶ ⟶ ⟶ ⟶ ⟶ ⟶

Be forward looking. Have you ever made a decision that seemed great in the moment but that turned out to have terrible consequences in the long run? (Yeah, sadly, me too.)

Now imagine that every person, every company, every government, and every nongovernmental organization in the world acted like that. The financial system would be in shambles, despots would be taking over vulnerable political regimes, and we'd all be experiencing an environmental crisis. Oh, wait, we're actually already there . . .

To be honest, previous generations of leaders have failed for the most part on this front, but we have an opportunity, *in this moment*, to right the course of history by thinking not just about the short-term payoffs from our choices but the long-term consequences as well. We can do this by implementing conservation and sustainability practices in our personal lives and by championing social and environmental responsibility in our work and our communities.

DO NOW ⟶ ⟶ ⟶ ⟶ ⟶ ⟶ ⟶ ⟶ ⟶

What social or environmental issue are you most interested in or do you want to learn more about? List three actions, beyond social media, you can take right now to help create a better future with regard to this issue. (For example, sign up to volunteer, subscribe to the newsletter for an organization that addresses this issue, invite a group of friends to go pick up trash at your neighborhood park, or even sign up for a race that supports an issue that you care about—perhaps the Hogwarts Running Club: www.hogwartsrunningclub.org.)   *(continued)*

An issue that I'm interested in or want to learn more about:

Three actions that I can take to help create a better future with regard to this issue:

Pick one, and do it! If necessary, set calendar reminders for any future actions.

Pay it forward. If you're one of the people who are lucky enough to have experienced success in your life and career, consider using what you've experienced and learned to lift others up and help push them forward. You can do this by mentoring or sponsoring people (and identifying them before they even come to you), by volunteering, or by donating to an organization that embodies your personal values. (See "Seeking Out and Maintaining Relationships with High-Quality People" under Chapter 2 of *The New Alpha Resource Guide* for more information on how to be an effective mentor.)

DO NOW

Make a list of at least five ways that you can "pay it forward." These should be actions that you can take that specifically benefit others (though you may also get some intrinsic reward from them):

Be the change. At the end of the day, people look to leaders as models for how to act, so if you want to build an ethical and effective organizational culture, then you have to model the behavior that you want to see. It really is that simple.

DO NOW →   →   →   →   →   →   →   →   →

Think of a time when you put the needs of the group or another person ahead of your own because it was the right thing to do. What was the situation? What did you do? Why did you do it? How did you feel afterward? How did the group respond? What did you learn from this experience that you will carry forward? Jot down your notes here:

The situation:

What I did:

Why I did this:

How I felt afterward:

How the group or person responded:

What I learned from this experience:

→   →   →   →   →   →   →   →   →   →   →   →

In closing this chapter, I leave you with words of wisdom from the ancient Greek philosopher Heraclitus: "Good character is not formed in a week or a month. It is created little by little, day by day." Be kind and patient with yourself, but keep moving in a forward direction.

WRAP-UP AND TRACKING PROGRESS

Step 1. Get Your *New Alpha Personal Excellence Tracker*

Download the *New Alpha Personal Excellence Tracker* from www.Leadership AndHumanPotential.com/Resources.

Step 2. Customize Your Tracker

Make a list of the character and ethics habits that you would like to focus on in your personal and/or professional life. These can be from the five listed in this chapter or others that you came up with on your own. Write these down here:

Next, adjust the "Demonstrate Character and Ethics" columns of the *New Alpha Personal Excellence Tracker* (these are the pink columns) to reflect the habits that you've identified. (Note that the five character and ethics habits from this chapter are already included, but you should edit, delete, or add to these to make them specific to your goals and needs.)

Step 3. Plan for Success

In the first column of the following chart, write out each of the character and ethics habits that you want to focus on further developing. You might identify habits that are already strengths or ones that you feel are relative areas of weakness for you. Be sure to give yourself a few lines of space in between each one.

In the second column, write out any obstacles that may make it difficult for you to adopt each of the habits that you listed in column 1 (for example, "I have a hard time standing up to authority figures, even when I know they're wrong."). In the third column, write out how you will overcome each of these obstacles (for example, "Each morning on the way to work, I will rehearse standing up to my supervisor.")

Character and Ethics Habits That I Want to Focus On	Potential Obstacles That I May Face	How I Will Overcome These Obstacles

Step 4. Track Your Progress

Make a note on your calendar or planner to *update your tracker every day*. You can do this by simply taking a moment to reflect on the day behind you. Did you have an opportunity to demonstrate any of the character and ethics habits that you're tracking? If so, put a 1 if you feel that you embodied the habit and 0 if you did not. Leave the cell blank if there were no opportunities to demonstrate a particular habit.

New Alpha Tip

Evaluating your own performance on various character and ethics habits can be tricky. Just do the best that you can, and try to be as honest as possible.

You can also print out a copy of your tracker if you find this easier than updating the spreadsheet version on your computer. Some people even like to import the tracker into a Google doc and then share it with a trusted friend or family member, so that they feel "accountable" to someone for keeping it up to date. Do what you need to do in order to customize this process to best fit your needs.

Step 5. Follow up and Continuously Improve

Make a note on your calendar or planner to do a weekly review of your progress (for example, every Sunday at 4 p.m.). This should only take 5 or 10 minutes max, and you'll need a pen and a notebook.

Use this time to review the data in your tracker for the past week, and write down any changes that you plan to make in order to increase the likelihood of accomplishing your goals. Even if you find yourself struggling with many or all of the habits that you chose to track from this chapter, I recommend focusing on no more than a total of one to two changes per week. This will allow you to master each habit more quickly, and eventually, you'll work through all of them. Don't get discouraged—I've been doing this for years, and I still fall short from time to time. Becoming a New Alpha is a marathon, not a sprint. As long as you put one foot in front of the other and keep pushing forward, you'll eventually end up exactly where you want to be—so it's worth being kind and flexible with yourself along the way.

Also, don't forget to celebrate progress and accomplishments! When you find yourself consistently taking advantage of opportunities to demonstrate character and ethics, be sure to take a moment to celebrate. (See "Celebrate the Small Wins" in Chapter 5, "Psychological and Organizational Strategies to Help You Achieve Your Goals," for more ideas and advice for how you can make this happen.)

Build Positive and Productive Relationships with Others

*People will forget what you said, people will forget what you
did, but people will never forget how you made them feel.*
—MAYA ANGELOU, American author,
poet, and civil rights activist

I'm not sure if you know this or not, but my grandma, Ruth Harlan, was kind of a big deal. I'm not saying this simply because she was my grandmother (or because her pies were the stuff of actual legends).[1] People loved that woman—and I mean **LOVED** in an all-caps, bold, no-holds-barred kind of way.

A small business owner for many years, even decades after she retired, former employees, colleagues, and business partners would visit from all over the world in order to share their appreciation for the positive impact that she'd had on their lives. In essence, she was the kind of person whom you just wanted to be around, and she was the kind of leader who walked the thin line with astonishing ease between being a goal-oriented go-getter and an inspiring people-person—and people couldn't get enough of her.

How'd she pull it off? Apart from being a competent businessperson, a thoughtful friend, and a genuinely kind person, she was exceptional at connecting with people and building positive and productive relationships.

So how exactly does one do this? How do we develop the kind of relationships that help us push the work forward *and* cultivate a sense of happiness and purpose in ourselves and the lives of others? The answer is, by focusing on, and building habits around, four major aims:

- Developing emotional intelligence
- Seeking out and maintaining relationships with high-quality people
- Understanding and leading effectively across lines of difference
- Minimizing time spent with toxic people

SELF-ASSESSMENT

The self-assessment in Table 2.1 will help you prioritize these aims for your needs and situation. For each question, check "True," "Depends or Not Sure," or "False." Then, we'll dive into them, one by one, and I'll provide suggestions for how you can turn them into habits that you use on a regular basis.

Table 2.1 **Self-Assessment Relationship Skills**

		True	Depends Or Not Sure	False
1	In general, I can recognize the emotions that I feel in different situations and identify them by name. (For example, I feel frustrated when I talk with my team members about budget issues.)			
2	I do not allow any moods or emotions that I am feeling to have a negative impact on my relationships with others.			
3	I can easily put myself in another's shoes in order to understand that person's perspective on a situation.			

		True	Depends Or Not Sure	False
4	I am good at motivating people toward a particular goal or course of action.			
5	I have people in my life whom I respect and/or look up to.			
6	I have people in my life who support me as a person and/or a professional.			
7	I have at least two or three people in my life whom I can turn to in times of extreme difficulty.			
8	I can identify at least one way that some aspect of my identity gives me power in certain social situations.			
9	I regularly use my power and influence in groups to make sure that everyone's voice is heard.			
10	In general, I do not spend time with people who drain my energy and/or make me feel badly about myself.			
11	I am good at setting boundaries, or even severing relationships, with people who drain my energy and/or make me feel badly about myself.			

Questions 1 through 4 correspond to the section of this chapter that covers *emotional intelligence*.

Questions 5 through 7 correspond to the section of this chapter that covers *seeking out and maintaining relationships with high-quality people*.

Questions 8 and 9 correspond to the section of this chapter that covers *understanding and leading effectively across lines of difference*.

Questions 10 and 11 correspond to the section of this chapter that covers *minimizing time spent with toxic people*.

Take note of any questions that you answered with "false" or "depends *or* not sure." Then look at the key below Table 2.1 to see which sections of this chapter correspond with those questions. These are the sections of this chapter that you should pay particular attention to.

DEVELOPING EMOTIONAL INTELLIGENCE

Emotional intelligence is the sine qua non of leadership.
—DANIEL GOLEMAN, author,
psychologist, and science journalist

Emotional intelligence (often abbreviated as EI or EQ) is the ability to recognize and effectively respond to our own emotions as well as those of others. Obviously, having strong emotional intelligence helps you build positive and productive relationships with others, but as a leader, your level of emotional intelligence can also affect everything from organizational performance to employee morale and productivity.[2]

If you look across the research on emotional intelligence, there's a lot of discussion about which competencies actually make up a person's EQ, but the model that I like best relates specifically to *emotional intelligence for leaders*, and it was first outlined by the psychologist Daniel Goleman, in the 1990s. The fact that most people are even familiar with the term *emotional intelligence* was largely due to his pioneering work in this area.

Over time, Goleman and his colleagues have done additional research and updated the original model, but in essence there are four main components to emotional intelligence: *self-awareness, self-management, social awareness, and relationship management.*[3]

Self-Awareness

Self-awareness refers to the ability to recognize your own emotions and motivations, as well as your strengths and limitations as a leader, and being aware of how these aspects of your personality or approach might be perceived by others.

For example, if you're feeling tired and cranky after a long day at work, recognizing this and politely telling your colleague that now is *not* the best time to discuss staffing projections for next year, and then graciously suggesting that you reschedule for another time, would be a typical example of this competency in action.

How to Make It Happen

Journal regularly—especially when you're feeling angry, frustrated, or upset. This will help you explore the emotions that you're feeling and recognize patterns of triggers, which is especially helpful for self-management, which we'll discuss in the next subsection.

I also like to go back and review my journal every few weeks. Doing so helps me see patterns of triggers and responses that I had no idea were occurring when I was in the moment but that provide useful insights for handling future situations that are similar.

For instance, if I am very hungry or tired, it's nearly impossible for me to have a productive intellectual debate that requires emotional self-control. Instead, I tend to get very frustrated and upset (some might even describe me as "hangry" during these moments . . .). Since I know this about myself, I take steps to ensure that I'm well fed and well rested before these types of conversations, and I delay them if they come up at an inopportune time.

Do *after-action reviews* of how you handle stressful interpersonal interactions. When you successfully navigate a stressful interaction with someone, think about what aspects of your personality, as could be seen in how you handled the situation, contributed to your success. When you have an interaction that doesn't go as well, reflect on what happened and what you might have done differently to produce a better outcome. Make notes about strategies that you would like to try if this situation comes up again, and make a best guess as to how they will play out.

If it's helpful, try to step out of your own "headspace," and imagine what someone whom you really like and respect would tell you to do in this type of situation. I do this all the time, and I swear, if I'm at all good at dealing with tricky interpersonal situations, it's because I've bombed so many of them and then imagined what someone like John Wooden (famous UCLA basketball coach, who led his team to 10 NCAA victories in 12 years) would tell me to do.

Think about a time when you felt highly motivated. What was the task or project, and why do you think you felt so motivated? Was your motivation related to something internal or to an outcome that you were excited about, or was there something about the situation or people with whom you were working that energized you?

For example, I have a friend who left his job to launch a new organization, but as a solo entrepreneur, he often found himself feeling bored and unmotivated with his work. Thinking back to past experiences in which he felt highly motivated and energetic about his work, he realized that he worked better with others around, so he enlisted a cofounder, and together they worked relentlessly to bring the organization to life.

Take a few self-assessments to get a better gauge of your personality and the strengths and pitfalls that go with it. For instance, I like the Myers-Briggs Type Indicator (MBTI)—it's not the end-all-be-all in terms of gauging your personality, but personally speaking, understanding my "best-fit" personality type (and what people with this type need to be aware of) has been really, really helpful in tailoring my approach to others.

For instance, since my natural tendency is to assert myself in most situations, I don't generally worry about voicing my opinion and making sure my ideas are heard. Instead, I think about when it would be most appropriate to assert myself (so that I don't come across as annoying or abrasive) and how I can ensure that everyone's voice is heard (using my assertiveness for good). Also, many employers will cover the cost of this assessment, so it's worth asking about if you're interested in taking it. (More information on the MBTI, and other useful assessments, is available in *The New Alpha Resource Guide*.)

Get feedback from others. Ask people whom you trust (family, close friends, coworkers, your boss) to identify the three best qualities that you bring to your relationships, organization, or role *as well as* your three most important areas for improvement, growth, and development. Just be sure to listen and *not argue* with any critical feedback that they have. Look, they may be totally off base and tell you that you need to improve on things that are totally B.S. If that's the case, you can always privately choose not to act on their feedback, but if you argue with everything they say, you'll only end up looking defensive and insecure. Just listen, get examples if necessary, and then do what you think is most appropriate with the information that they share with you.

Self-Management

Self-management refers to the ability to control and redirect any disruptive emotions or impulses you experience so that you can stay focused and energetic and help others around you do the same. This competency would be relevant, for example, when your boss drops an important project "due by Monday" on your desk at 3 p.m. on Friday.

Self-management doesn't mean that you don't feel angry or frustrated in situations like this or that you shouldn't speak up or try to make improvements. It simply means that you don't act on that first primal impulse to launch your phone at your boss's head and then throw your body onto the floor in a spectacular show of emotion (at least not while she's still in the room).

How to Make It Happen

Create some space. If possible, find a way to create some temporary distance between you and the person who's causing you to get bent out of shape. Get some fresh air, go for a walk or run, write in your journal, and do what you need to do in order to calm down and remain level-headed. If you're in a situation with another person who's frustrating you and demanding a response, feel free to tell that person that you need some time to think about what he or she has said and you'll respond as soon as you've done so.

Distract yourself with a thinking task. This one sounds weird, but I got the idea from one of my favorite shows: *Jane the Virgin*. In this show, when Jane gets frustrated or raging mad, her grandmother tells her to turn the word *calma* (Spanish for "calm") into an acronym of words that she finds calming and soothing.

So for me, this would be *cuddling, aerobics, Luna* (my cat), *Mom*, and *altruism*: CALMA. It sounds weird (and nerdy beyond belief), but actually taking the time to think of five words that start with the letters CALMA always calms me down. Making yourself engage in this kind of "thinking task" forces your immediate focus out of the "emotional" reptilian area of your brain and back into the executive and logical area that makes good decisions.

Try breathing exercises. If you find yourself feeling frustrated, angry, or some other strong and negative emotion, try breathing in through your

nostrils for four counts, holding for four counts, exhaling through your nostrils for six counts, and then holding again for two counts. Like this:

- Breath in (four counts)
- Hold breath (four counts)
- Exhale (six counts)
- Hold (two counts)

I learned this trick from the Art of Living Foundation, and it totally works! (For more information on the Art of Living, see "Manage Stress" under Chapter 3 in *The New Alpha Resource Guide*.)

Remember: Self-management is powerful. Even if it feels awful and painful while you're doing it (which it very often does), it almost always produces a better outcome that allows you to maintain or increase your power and influence in the long run. Personally, this is my weakest area of emotional intelligence, but it is also the one that I almost never see a New Alpha leader without.

Social Awareness

People with *social awareness* can recognize the (spoken and unspoken) moods and emotions of others, and they are able to assess situations from multiple perspectives. In other words, they are *empathetic*.

For example, if you have a colleague or teammate who is usually on time with everything but who is suddenly late on a project, using this competency might entail pausing to think about or ask if there is something going on in that person's life that might be affecting her or his work (for example, a sick relative or a big move) before deciding how to deal with the situation.

How to Make It Happen

Pay attention to people's body language and energy levels—especially any recent changes. Is someone who's usually upright and outspoken, suddenly slumped and quiet when you meet with her? If so, ask if there's anything going on that she'd like to talk about. Similarly, pay attention to people's other nonverbal signals and facial cues. Is the person sighing deeply, not making eye contact, or smiling without showing his teeth? These are often powerful clues about how they are feeling.

If you want to learn more, the Greater Good Science Center, based at UC Berkeley, has an in-depth quiz that will help you assess your abilities here and understand how to read nonverbal cues. See *The New Alpha Resource Guide* for more information and a link to the quiz.

Periodically check in and follow up with people. If someone mentions a recent life event or change (for example, a parent coming to visit, an engagement, or the death of a loved one), make a note of it, and remind yourself to follow up as necessary.

Since I tend to be ridiculously overscheduled and bad at keeping track of these things in my head, if a friend, family member, or coworker mentions something like this to me, I set a reminder on my calendar to follow up in a few days. I recognize that this seems very calculating and contrived, but I also feel like it's better than my forgetting and the person's feeling like I don't care about her. It's also one less thing for my frenetic brain to worry about remembering, which helps me to more effectively manage my stress levels.

If you're confused or not sure how someone is feeling, ask him. If you're worried that the person might not be comfortable sharing his feelings in a public setting, arrange to meet with him privately. You can just say something like, "Hey, I noticed that you seem [insert emotion that you think you're seeing], and I was just wondering if I'm correct here? If so, I want you to know that I'm here if there's something that you want to talk about." Then stop talking and simply wait for him to respond.

Unless, the person is super private (or just really passive aggressive), he will usually share with you what's going on (and it might be exactly what you suspect—or something totally different). Even if the person *is* acting passive aggressively, he'll usually knock it off once you kindly call his behavior out in this way. If it continues and if he swears nothing is wrong, then at least you can rest easy knowing that you did your best to understand and resolve the situation. The rest may very well just be something that he has to work through on his own or without your help.

Listen to what people say—without interrupting. If there were one skill that I wish I were better at, it would be listening. Just keeping your mouth shut and listening to people can do wonders!

In my case, my nature is to be super inquisitive and very oriented toward problem solving. But I've learned that *most of the time*, if I just resist the urge to speak, and actually listen, people will often talk or vent their way from describing their problem to developing a workable solution *on their own, and without my help*—which is another win-win-win situation. In other words, they resolved their problem, *and* because they came up with the solution on their own, they feel empowered and are more likely to actually implement the solution. Plus, they value you because you sat there and listened while they talked it out.

Really, being a good listener is more difficult than I'm making it sound, but it is worth trying. (See "Emotional Intelligence" under Chapter 3 *The New Alpha Resource Guide* for more ideas here.)

Put yourself in the other person's shoes. Sometimes people are late, don't deliver on what they promise, or forget things because they are selfish and evil, but most of the time, I've found that there's a totally acceptable reason for someone's lack of performance, and if I can just pause for a moment and imagine myself in her situation, 9 times out of 10, I can figure out why the problem is occurring and how to fix it.

The next time you feel angry, frustrated, or disappointed by someone, force yourself to make a case for why she did what she did. Now, this doesn't mean that you should let people get away with what is clearly bad, disrespectful, and/or unethical behavior, but if you put yourself in the other person's shoes first, you're more likely to come up with a solution that's reasonable *and* effective in the long run.

Be there for people who need a shoulder to cry on. Sometimes, people feel so overwhelmed or stressed or sad that the mere act of someone's asking how they're doing can open a floodgate of emotions and even tears. In fact, this happened to me the other day with a student: I sensed that she was feeling stressed and upset, so I asked her how she was feeling, and she just started bawling.

Raise your hand if this has ever happened to you. If you've never experienced it, this kind of behavior may seem odd or unprofessional, but it can actually be a sign that the person who's opening up trusts you enough to reveal the most vulnerable aspects of himself, and that's a good thing. Even if you feel awkward about it, do what you need to do to listen and comfort him. Depending on the situation, this may entail simply nodding to show that you understand what he is saying, handing him a tissue or a drink of water, patting him on the back, or a even giving him a hug if it's someone

with whom you have a close relationship. (FYI: I recommend this last option only if there's absolutely no chance that your overture will be misper-
ceived by the other person.)

Relationship Management

Relationship management is all about the ability to use *self-awareness*,
self-management, and *social awareness* to influence and motivate people
toward a goal. Daniel Goleman calls it "friendliness with a purpose."[4]
This competency is especially relevant to persuasion, collaboration, and
conflict management—which are all skills that are essential for effective
leadership.

My friend James Bond, a University of Maryland administrator, is
an all-star on this aspect of EQ. Whether he's bringing together campus
leaders to improve student government, rallying people to raise money
for a good cause (he's on the board of a local nonprofit that works to fight
homelessness), or convincing friends to join him in a 10K race across the
Maryland Bay Bridge, James has a knack for connecting disparate groups
of people and uniting them as a force for good.

I first met James when we were students at the University of Maryland where he was an important mentor to me, and he introduced me to
many of the people from college with whom I'm still friends today. Given
his knack for relationship management, it's no surprise that during our
student days, he was student government president, Mr. Maryland, outstanding student of the year, and winner of the best citizen award. When
you're as good as James is at building relationships, connecting people, and
moving them toward a common goal, you also tend to be pretty successful.

How to Make It Happen

Use your empathy. Before explaining a project or task to someone, put
yourself in her shoes and imagine what would be most motivating for her.
Use this information to tailor your communication in the way that's most
likely to inspire and engage her. The ability to do this regularly is a lot like
snowboarding: difficult to learn, but easy to master once you get the hang
of it.

Embrace group work. Recognize that no matter how competent you are,
if you want to do something big, you're going to need other people's help.

In one of my favorite episodes of the show *30 Rock*, Al Gore says, "There's an old African proverb that says, 'If you want to go quickly, go alone. If you want to go far, go together.'" True that, Mr. Vice President!

Learn to give and take. The best piece of negotiation advice that I ever got is this: in a good negotiation, everyone gives something and everyone gets something. What I've learned over time is that, more than just being a nice result, this type of outcome tends to increase commitment on both sides and lead to more trusting relationships, which saves a lot of time and energy in the long run.

Observe people. Identify two to three people in your life who you think are exceptionally strong at relationship management (like my friend, James Bond!). List them here:

1.

2.

3.

DO NOW → → → → → → → → →

Make an appointment to meet with each of those people for drinks, lunch, coffee, or something else, and get their views on relationship management, including any advice that they have for doing this effectively. In some cases, when you find people who are really good at this, they've done it for so long that it might feel "innate" to them.

For these people, relationship management is more of an unconscious habit than a conscious action. So, rather than asking for step-by-step instructions, try asking for their "philosophy" around relationship management or their "approach" to building and maintaining positive and productive relationships. Make note of any key takeaways from these conversations here:

Keep learning! The ability to effectively persuade, collaborate, and manage conflict is largely based not on any special gifts or talents but on skills that are learned over time and through personal experience. If you want to hit the ground running when these situations arise in your life, keep an eye out for coaching opportunities, courses, workshops, books, and articles that will help you to increase your competency here. Many workplaces will even pay for specialized training, especially if you can show how it will improve your performance at work.

SEEKING OUT AND MAINTAINING RELATIONSHIPS WITH HIGH-QUALITY PEOPLE

*Surround yourself with only people
who are going to lift you higher.*
—Oprah Winfrey, American media proprietor,
talk show host, actress, producer, and philanthropist

Beyond working to develop and increase your EQ, it's also important to find and keep high-quality people in your life. High-quality people are those who have a positive influence and help you develop into your best self. There are a couple of ways that you can cultivate these relationships:

1. Develop a circle of support.

2. Be proactive.

3. Be gracious and helpful.

4. Keep in touch and let people know how much you appreciate and value their presence in your life.

Develop a Circle of Support

A *circle of support* is a group of people who provide you with various types of support when you need it. Obviously, you might have one or more "go-to" people for support with typical or everyday issues, but a circle of support involves a number of people across key areas to ensure that, no matter what the situation—career related, family related, emotional, intellectual, or something else—you always have someone whom you can count on. Having a circle of support also means that you don't have to rely on a single person to fulfill all of your needs—however romantic this idea may seem.

There's no one best way to develop your circle of support—and I don't recommend formally asking people to join (awkward . . .). Instead, when you meet high-quality people who you want to keep in your life, be sure to keep in touch with them, give more than you get, and let them know how much you appreciate their support.

Build a Circle of Support

A circle of support isn't built up over night. Cultivating and nurturing these relationships requires effort and time. (It's taken me about 20 years to build mine!) Below are the types of people you want to have on your side:

- **Inspirers** are people who inspire and motivate you to be your best self.

- **Mentors** are people whom you can go to for advice and guidance (personal or professional). They're often your "sounding boards."

- **Sponsors** are like mentors, but they're more invested in you, so they regularly champion you and your work and recommend you for opportunities. They may also see you as their protégé.

- **Reliables** are people who are reliable and always there for you.

- **Emotional supporters** are close friends with whom you can be your most raw and authentic self.

- **True peers** are people who share similar experiences, ways of thinking, and even challenges.

- **Challengers** are people who aren't afraid to push back and give you constructive feedback when it's necessary.

DO NOW → → → → → → → → →

Now that you know a bit more about the types of people that you want in your circle of support, take a moment to quickly jot down the people in your current circle of support, and those who could potentially be in your circle at some point in the future (indicating the "potentials" with an asterisk (*) by their name). Keep in mind that you can have more than one person in each category.

Inspirers:

Mentors:

Sponsors:

Reliables:

Emotional supporters:

True peers:

Challengers:

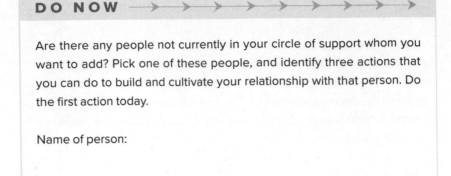

DO NOW →→ →→ →→ →→ →→ →→ →→ →

Are there any people not currently in your circle of support whom you want to add? Pick one of these people, and identify three actions that you can do to build and cultivate your relationship with that person. Do the first action today.

Name of person:

Three actions that I can take to cultivate a relationship with this person:

Be Proactive

If you identify a high-quality person with whom you'd like to build a relationship, don't wait for him to make the first move. Ask him out for coffee, invite him on a walk, or offer to help him with a project.

New Alpha Tip

Be mindful about *how* you approach people. It's easy for innocent overtures to be misinterpreted, so make it clear (without inadvertently making the other person feel uncomfortable) that you're reaching out in a purely friendly or professional way—for example, by making it a group get-together, rather than a one-on-one interaction.

If you don't know this person well, ask for an introduction from a mutual acquaintance or send him an email to introduce yourself and ask if he has time to meet and chat. If you don't already have his contact information, you can often find it by doing a quick Google search.

Here's an example of how to word your email:

> Hi X,
>
> I hope you're doing well and having a great week! I am emailing you (a) to introduce myself—[insert name and title or other relevant identifier here]—and (b) because I'm interested in your work on [insert work of interest here], and I wanted to see if you have some time in the next few weeks to grab coffee and talk more about your experiences, including any advice that you might have for someone interested in this topic.
>
> Please let me know if you are available.
>
> Thanks so much!
>
> Me

Obviously, you'll want to tailor this to meet your specific needs (and to be in your voice, not mine), but short, sweet, and to the point is best. If you don't get a response within a week or two, send a courteous follow-up. Bonus points if you also include a resource that might be relevant or helpful to him, such as a journal or newspaper article that's positively related to his work.

Don't get discouraged if not every person responds to your requests—some are going to pan out and some aren't. The point is that you will never know unless you put yourself out there and initiate contact.

DO NOW → → → → → → → →

Who's someone whom you admire and would like to get to know better, but are nervous about contacting? If you could meet him, what is the number one question that you'd like to ask him? If you haven't already done this, contact him through email right now. Jot down your notes from the experience in the space below.

(continued)

> ## New Alpha Tip
>
> It's also okay (and maybe even preferable) to pick someone who's not world famous but whom you personally admire—these people are often the most accessible and helpful.

Name of person:

My question for this person:

Date reached out:

Outcome:

Next steps:

Be Gracious and Helpful

Having a strong network of awesome people who support you is a great thing, but as Adam Grant reminds us in his bestselling book *Give and Take*, the most successful people tend to be those who give more than they take.[5] (True to what he preaches, Adam Grant and his colleague Reb Rebele were kind enough to dig up a number of useful resources that I referenced when writing this chapter.)

Keep in mind that high-achieving people are often incredibly busy, so if you seek someone out for advice, support, friendship, or whatever it may be, just make sure that you're being gracious and respectful of her time and that you're being helpful. Making it easy to meet or offering to help on a project goes a long way.

Even if you can't offer the same level of support that the other person brings to the relationship, try to offer something. You can do this by buying her a cup of coffee, sending her an article or resource that's relevant to one of her current projects, offering to introduce her to someone whom she might want in her network, or asking her how you can be helpful and supportive of her goals and aspirations. Speaking from my own experience as someone who both reaches out for support a lot *and* who gets a lot of requests: a little effort on your part can signal a lot to someone who's constantly being bombarded with people asking for her time, help, or advice.

In the case of the people who mentor you: over time, as the mentoring relationship develops into friendship, the relationship becomes less one-sided, but it's important in the beginning—especially if you're the one who's initiating the relationship—to ensure that you're doing your part to add value for the other person. That doesn't mean that you'll actually accomplish this—just that you're trying your best not to be a self-centered mooch.

At the very least, *always* be sure to thank your mentors for their time, support, and advice—even if nothing tangible is being exchanged. People who are frequently in demand are more likely to prefer helping those who are gracious and respectful about their time.

New Alpha Tip

Handwritten thank-you cards, in addition to thank-you emails sent within 24 hours, really make people stand out in a good way.

DO NOW

In what ways do you give more than you take? How can you bring value to your relationships? Some examples include: being a good listener, being gracious, offering to help with something that you're good at, and making productive connections between people in your network. List your ideas here:

Keep in Touch and Let People Know How Much You Appreciate and Value Their Presence in Your Life

Too often, we fall out of contact with high-quality people because we move or get busy or we feel like we've let too much time go by, but there are at least two big reasons why this is a mistake.

First, as you move along in life and constantly strive to better yourself, you'll eventually notice that the truly high-quality people are not actually that common. So, if you happen to be lucky enough to come across one in your life, it makes sense to hold onto that person.

Second, it's actually pretty easy to keep in touch, and doing so doesn't necessarily mean a lot of time-consuming planning or elaborate strategy on your part. There are some people in my life with whom I speak only once or twice a year and that's more than enough. The point is that I make an effort to keep good relationships going.

How to Make It Happen

- If you struggle to know whom to keep in touch with and how often to do so, try keeping a list of the people from your circle of support and others who bring you joy and/or help you to be the best version of yourself. Then set a weekly or monthly reminder to pick one or two people from the list to reach out to. This may feel overly planned and forced at first, but over time, you'll start to internalize this list of people, and it will become second nature to reach out to them. (I'm thinking of one right now even as I type this . . .)

- Keep track of people's birthdays by adding them to your online calendar and classifying them as repeating yearly events, and when the time comes, send them a card with a personalized note. (By now you've realized that I heart calendar reminders! They're like this super-easy-but-little-known secret to big success.)

- If you come across an article, resource, or even a job posting that is relevant to someone you know, send him a quick email to say hello and share the link. It takes less than 60 seconds to do, and it is a powerful way to reinforce the relationship bond.

- If you're out and happen to see something that makes you smile and think of a particular person (like her favorite slogan on a poster), then snap a picture and send her a text explaining that it reminded you of her. (Be mindful that this is generally more appropriate for people with whom you have a close and friendly relationship.)

- In the event that you haven't talked to someone in a long time, send him an email apologizing for all the time that's gone by and asking him how he's been. I've done this many times after years of not talking with a friend or colleague, and I have yet to receive any response other than that the person was glad to hear from me.

By keeping in touch with high-quality people and letting them know that they're genuinely valued and appreciated, you'll strengthen your relationships and increase your feelings of joy, connectedness, and fulfillment.

DO NOW → → → → → → → → → → →

List three to five things that you can do to let the high-quality people in your life know how much you value and appreciate them:

Pick one of these, and do it right now!

UNDERSTANDING AND LEADING EFFECTIVELY
ACROSS LINES OF DIFFERENCE

Make a career of humanity, commit yourself to the noble
struggle for equal rights. You will make a greater person
of yourself, a greater nation of your country,
and a finer world to live in.
—MARTIN LUTHER KING, JR.,
American Baptist minister, activist, humanitarian, and
leader in the African-American civil rights movement

Whether we like it or not, there are certain aspects of our identity that affect how people perceive us, and thus, the amount of social power that we enjoy.[6] In the modern world, multiple aspects of a person's identity intersect and interact with one another to affect the overall level of social privilege or penalty that the person experiences. These include factors such as age, race, ethnicity, gender and gender identity, sexual orientation, wealth, job title, religion, work experience, geographic location, appearance, income, education, language, and physical ability, among others. In some cases, a person might be privileged by some aspects of their identity (for example, straight, white, . . .) and penalized by other aspects (for example, poor, female, . . .).[7]

Oftentimes, people get really uptight when they're reminded of their privilege, but in reality, for the most part, privilege isn't something that any one person can decide to have or not have. In most cases, you're born with, or into, it—and having it certainly doesn't make you a bad person. (Personally, I've got loads of it, especially of the white variety . . .). However, if you are privileged by one or more aspects of your identity, it's important to recognize this and use it for good (rather than just pretending it doesn't exist). You can do this by taking proactive steps to ensure that everyone's voice is being heard and correcting negative, disrespectful, or marginalizing behavior when you see it (even if it's not directed at you).

Ultimately, our goal as the rising generation of leaders is to shape our society into one in which different groups of people are neither privileged nor penalized based on their particular identities. Since we're not there yet though, it would be a mistake to overlook or feign ignorance about the problems around us. Instead, our role is to recognize inequality when we see it and to actively choose to be a part of the solution, rather than perpetuating a system of oppression that we're a part of whether we want to be or not.[8]

How to Make It Happen

Do some self-reflection. What aspects of your identity *could* be a source of privilege in certain situations? For instance, I taught a course at Stanford with a (white male) mentor of mine who's several decades older and a tenured professor. In some ways, my identity gave me more power as an instructor (for example, students tended to open up to me more quickly and more often than they did with him), and in some ways his identity gave him more power as an instructor (for example, students were less likely to quibble with him about their grade on an assignment). Though we shared the same racial identity, I learned a lot by seeing how the other aspects of our identities (such as age, gender, seniority, and tenure status) affected how others related to us.

DO NOW

Use the space below to identify any aspects of your identity that might be a source of privilege in certain situations:

Educate yourself on the issues. Whether you experience discrimination in your daily life or not (and many of us do), the fact is that prejudicial attitudes and (even unintentional) discriminatory behavior are pervasive, and large numbers of people across our communities and around the globe are routinely targeted because of one or more aspects of their social identity.

Of all the people I know who try to keep up with what's going on in the world, the people whom I see doing this the best are those who *proactively* explore and engage with the issues. Beyond just being active on social media, they make an effort to read books that address the issues that they care about, they talk with other smart and thoughtful people, they visit and work in communities and countries other than their own, they read the news (from a variety of sources with different political leanings, to control for bias), and they support causes that they believe in (by volunteering, protesting, writing letters, making calls, and donating money).

These folks aren't perfect—from time to time, they make mistakes and have to apologize—but they're okay with getting uncomfortable, and they act humbly and in the spirit of continuous improvement and learning. Personally speaking, I've put my foot in my mouth more than once when discussing sensitive issues around equality and lines of difference, and I've found that a simple and heartfelt apology is all it usually takes to get my foot out of my mouth.

DO NOW → → → → → → → → → →

Think about the social identities that are often penalized in our society. Which of these do you know the least about, or which seems the most different from your own identity? How can you find out more about this identity? Are there books or academic papers that you can read? What about documentaries? What about volunteer work? What else? List the identity that you're interested in learning more about and your ideas for learning more about this topic here.

(By the way, I did this activity in order to learn more about people who identify as transgender, and it was incredibly helpful and informative—and made me feel like a much stronger ally.)

I'm interested in learning more about people who...

Actions that I can take to increase my understanding of this topic:

New Alpha Tip

Just because you have a friend who's Latino, gay, deaf, or some-thing else doesn't mean that you are entitled to use her as your en-cyclopedia of what it's like to have that social identity. Some people are more than happy to share their experiences with others, but you shouldn't assume that everyone is—or that those who are comfort-able sharing can accurately speak for everyone with that identity.

Pay attention, speak up, be proactive. Think about the people in your cur-rent work or organization. Are there voices that aren't being heard, per-haps because they're not being given the opportunity to speak, or because they're being cut off, or perhaps even because of seemingly minute actions or attitudes on the part of other group members that might be making these people feel marginalized?

DO NOW ⟶ ⟶ ⟶ ⟶ ⟶ ⟶ ⟶ ⟶ ⟶

Think about an example of intentional bigotry (intolerant behavior or re-marks) or unintentional discrimination (for example, women repeatedly being talked over or interrupted in situations in which men are not) that you recently experienced or witnessed. Answer the following questions:

What was the situation?

What actions did you take, if any?

(continued)

What was the outcome of the situation?

Were you satisfied with the outcome? Why or why not?

What would you do differently next time? (It's okay to be honest here. I have yet to experience a moment of my standing up for myself or someone else that I think went perfectly, but that doesn't stop me from reflecting on my mistakes and thinking about how I could do better in the future. Remember, the goal is to continuously improve over time.)

Be a part of the solution. According to everyone from Voltaire to Uncle Ben (Spiderman's uncle), with great power, privilege, and/or social position comes great responsibility.[9] More than just recognizing and speaking out when we see behavior that unfairly discriminates against or marginalizes people, we must correct this kind of behavior when we see it (even if it feels uncomfortable to do so), and we must put structures and processes in place that prevent it from happening. As the new movement of *influencers* and *changemakers*, it is our responsibility to explicitly and proactively send the message that penalizing people because of their identity (whether intentional or not) is never okay.

We are the owners of tomorrow, so let's use our privilege for good. If we don't stand up for what's right, who else will?

For additional resources on leading effectively across lines of difference, see *The New Alpha Resource Guide*.

MINIMIZING TIME SPENT WITH TOXIC PEOPLE

> *Crazymakers like drama. If they can swing it, they are*
> *the star. Everyone around them functions as supporting cast,*
> *picking up their cues, their entrances and exits,*
> *from the crazymaker's (crazy) whims.*
> —JULIA CAMERON, American teacher, author,
> artist, poet, playwright, novelist, filmmaker,
> composer, and journalist

Have you ever spent time with someone and felt completely drained and/ or like crap about yourself afterward? Sure, we all have those moments in which we fail to act like the best version of ourselves, but some people are consistently narcissistic, overly needy or dependent, belligerent, or total run-of-the-mill [insert your favorite expletive noun here]. In essence, these people are *toxic*.

If you're like me, you might try to have the old "When you [insert bad behavior here], I feel [insert negative emotion here]" conversation to identify and help correct his bad behavior—and sometimes this works. If so, kudos to you! But in my experience, truly toxic people rarely respond to even the most well-intentioned and psychologically healthy interventions. If you happen to find yourself dealing with one of these gems, then your best strategy is to minimize the amount of time that you have to spend with him.

Sometimes this is easy. You can be honest with the person about how she makes you feel and then cut her off if she can't or won't change her behavior. Other times, you can't actually be honest and directly cut the toxic person off because he's likely to respond with extreme aggression and/or insane drama. This, of course, puts you in a catch-22: you dread spending time with this person, but you're not willing to incur the wrath that will almost certainly result from your being brutally honest about pulling back from the relationship.

If you're ever in this situation, it's totally acceptable to find yourself conveniently busy with other things whenever the toxic person wants to hang out. Eventually, even if she doesn't fully understand what is happening or why, she will realize that you're no longer available to put up with her abuse, and she will stop making overtures.

If you're in the unfortunate situation in which you can't avoid spending time with the toxic person—maybe you work with him or he is a family member who attends all of the same family events—then do your best to ignore him. While this advice never seemed to work with middle school bullies, it's surprising how brilliantly it works in the grown-up world.

Toxic people thrive by forcing their negative emotions onto others, so if they see that this tactic doesn't work with you, they'll eventually stop or move on to someone else. Every once in a while they'll even apologize once they've stopped getting a reaction from you. The point is this: life is short—you can't be everything to everyone. Know your own worth, and choose to spend your time with high-quality people who value and appreciate what you bring to the table.

DO NOW → → → → → → → → →

Make a list of the toxic people in your life. Remember, these aren't necessarily people whom you don't like or whom you argue the most with; rather, they are people who consistently drain your energy and make you feel badly about yourself:

Fill out the chart in Table 2.2 about the *most challenging* toxic person in your life. (I've provided an example first.)

Table 2.2 **Toxic People**

Name of Toxic Person	Example of Toxic Behavior	How This Person Makes Me Feel	Reasons Why I Spend Time with This Person	Steps That I Can Take to Minimize Time I Spend with This Person
Cara	She refuses to attend group lunch unless she picks the restaurant, then complains the entire time, and sends everyone an offensive email afterward saying how awful the lunch was.	I feel frustrated, angry, and confused, as if logic doesn't work.	She is part of an annual group luncheon that involves many people I care about; sometimes I feel guilty when she reaches out because she's sad or lonely.	I can be polite when I see her at events like the annual luncheon, but I avoid going to see her when she invites me to visit her (because I feel that this sends the message that I'm okay with her bad behavior). If I feel guilty, I can send her an email rather than visit.

WRAP-UP AND TRACKING PROGRESS

Step 1. Open Your *New Alpha Personal Excellence Tracker*

Open up your *New Alpha Personal Excellence Tracker* (which you downloaded in the "Wrap-Up and Tracking Progress" section of the previous chapter).

Step 2. Customize Your Tracker

Make a list of any of the habits covered in this chapter that you would like to focus on in your personal and/or professional life. These can be ones that were explicitly stated or others that you came up with on your own. Write these down here:

Next, adjust the "Build Positive and Productive Relationships with Others" columns of the *New Alpha Personal Excellence Tracker* (these are the orange columns) to reflect the habits that you've identified. (Note that the main aims from this chapter that you want to develop into habits are already included, but you should edit, delete, or add to these to make them specific to your goals and needs. In my opinion, these are some of the most complex habits in this part of the book, so feel free to break them down into smaller pieces if that's helpful.)

Step 3. Plan for Success

In the first column of the following chart, write out each of the habits from this chapter that you want to focus on, giving yourself a few lines of space in between each one. In the second column, write out any obstacles that may hinder you from success with a particular habit (for example, "The toxic person in my life is a colleague whom I see regularly"). In the third column, write out how you will overcome each of these obstacles (for example, "I will make a daily note to avoid starting conversations with this person").

Habits of Positive and Productive Relationships That I Want to Focus On	Potential Obstacles That I May Face	How I Will Overcome These Obstacles

Step 4. Track Your Progress

Continue to *update your tracker every day.* As always, do what you need to do in order to customize this process to best fit your needs.

Step 5. Follow up and Continuously Improve

Continue to review your tracker weekly. Take a look at the data in your tracker for the past week, and use a notebook to write down any changes that you plan to make in order to increase your likelihood of adopting a particular habit. Remember that the goal is continuous improvement over time, so don't be too hard on yourself if you're not yet where you want to be—you'll get there eventually. In the meantime, keep celebrating progress in the right direction.

Prioritize Your Health and Wellness

To keep the body in good health is a duty [. . .]; otherwise we shall not be able to keep our mind strong and clear.
—BUDDHA, Eastern sage on whose teachings Buddhism was founded

Early on in my career, I had a colleague, whom I'll call Sara, who was a rock star among rock stars when it came to her job. Her ethics were flawless, her management was impeccable, and walking into one of her team meetings was something akin to walking into Hogwarts—magical and exciting. Sara worked days, nights, and weekends to be the best team member she could be, sacrificing things like sleep and exercise, in pursuit of the best results possible.

The problem? Over time, Sara began to have serious health issues—her immunity weakened, and she started getting sick . . . a lot. She missed several months of work, gained 20 pounds in a year, and was diagnosed with high blood pressure (in her twenties and with no family history of the disease). She also started to withdraw from her friends and colleagues, and eventually she confided in a few of us that she was suffering from clinical depression.

Her doctor's theory? She simply wasn't taking good enough care of herself to sustain the level of energy required to do the kind of work that she was doing.

In my experience, Sara's story is a common one. The problem is: though often underemphasized in the traditional Alpha model, prioritizing your health and wellness is *essential* for anyone who wants to live a good life, achieve success, *and* make a difference in the world. Too often, people with big goals put self-care last—to the detriment of their well-being *and* their long-term ability to have an impact on the issues they care about.

This chapter begins with a self-assessment that will help you to determine which areas of health and wellness you'll want to focus on further developing in your life as you travel on your New Alpha path. Then, relying on real-world examples and science-based recommendations, we'll lay out some healthy (and realistic) habits around eating well, staying hydrated, getting enough sleep, exercising regularly, and effectively managing stress.

SELF-ASSESSMENT

Depending on your current level of health and wellness, certain sections in this chapter may be more or less useful to you. Use this self-assessment to identify which sections you should prioritize.

1. How often do you eat from each of the major food groups (fruits; vegetables; whole grains; protein, nuts, legumes; and dairy or dairy alternatives)?

   A. I regularly eat from one or two of these food groups on a daily basis.

   B. I regularly eat from three or four of these food groups on a daily basis.

   C. I regularly eat foods from all of these food groups on a daily basis.

2. Tug at the skin between your thumb and forefinger. How quickly does it bounce back?

   A. Hmmm . . . now that I think about it, it does seem to take a while to bounce back.

   B. It bounces back almost immediately.

   C. It bounces back immediately.

3. On average, how alert do you feel throughout the day?

   A. On most days, I feel sluggish and inattentive throughout the day.

   B. Sometimes, I feel tired during the day, but it depends on what's going on in my life.

   C. I have my moments, but in general, I'm fairly alert throughout the day.

4. How often do you exercise or get some form of physical activity in your day?

   A. I rarely exercise (two or fewer times per week).

   B. I exercise at least a few (three to four) times per week.

   C. I exercise every (or almost every) day.

5. How do you feel about the amount of stress in your life?

   A. I have some stress in my life, but I feel like I am easily able to manage it.

   B. I have some stress in my life, and I'd like to more effectively recognize and manage it.

   C. My life is very stressful, and I would love some strategies for dealing with it more effectively.

6. How often do you eat processed (pre-prepared or not from-scratch) meals? (This includes eating out or ordering in.)

   A. One or more times per day.

   B. A few (three to four) times per week.

   C. Never. I'm a total gourmand and cook everything from scratch.

7. How often do you experience the following afflictions: headache, constipation, or dry skin?

   A. Frequently (I experience two or more of these each week).

   B. Regularly (I usually experience one of these each week).

   C. Rarely (I experience some of these sometimes, but I wouldn't say they are common occurrences for me).

8. How do you feel about your sleep habits?

    A. I feel pretty good about my sleep habits—they may not be perfect, but I think I'm getting enough high-quality sleep to function well throughout the day.

    B. There are probably one or two changes that I should make (for example, set a regular bedtime, get a few additional minutes of shut-eye each night), but in general, I feel okay about my sleep habits.

    C. Yikes—I'm constantly tired, sluggish, and/or cranky, and I'm pretty sure I need more (and better!) sleep.

9. If you are physically able to exercise, what is your fitness focus: endurance and cardio, flexibility, and/or strength? (Skip this question if you cannot exercise because of health reasons or if your doctor has already prescribed a particular exercise regimen to meet your specific fitness needs.)

    A. When I exercise, I mainly focus on one of these fitness goals.

    B. When I exercise, I mainly focus on two of these fitness goals (though not necessarily in the same session).

    C. When I exercise, I regularly focus on all three of these fitness goals (though not necessarily in the same session).

10. How many strategies can you identify right now that you regularly use to successfully manage the stress in your life?

    A. I can identify one or two strategies that I regularly use to successfully mange the stress in my life.

    B. I can identify at least three strategies that I regularly use to successfully manage the stress in my life.

    C. I can't think of any particularly useful strategies that I regularly use to successfully manage the stress in my life.

11. How would you describe your eating habits?

    A. I eat a healthy and well-balanced diet some of the time.

    B. I rarely eat a healthy and well-balanced diet.

    C. I eat a healthy and well-balanced diet all of the time.

12. How thirsty are you right now?

    A. Come to think of it, I'm *very* thirsty right now—hold on while I go get some water.

    B. Hmm . . . I might be kind of thirsty right now, since you mention it.

    C. I'm not thirsty right now. I feel very well hydrated.

13. On average, how much sleep do you get each night?

    A. Fewer than seven hours.

    B. Seven to nine hours.

    C. More than nine hours.

14. Excepting any long-term physical disabilities that may impact your fitness and strength, how do you feel about your current level of physical fitness?

    A. I wish I were more physically fit and/or there are several activities in my day that are physically hard for me to do.

    B. I feel strong and fit enough to do most or all of my daily activities, though there may be some room for improvement.

    C. I feel strong and fit enough to do most or all of my daily activities.

15. How quickly do you recognize when you're stressed out?

    A. I am usually quick to recognize when I'm feeling stressed out.

    B. I am sometimes quick to recognize when I'm feeling stressed out.

    C. By the time I recognize that I'm feeling stressed, it's almost always too late (for example, I feel completely out of control and overwhelmed *or* I become physically ill).

YOUR RESULTS

You can check your results in Table 3.1. Make a note of any categories on which you scored 7 or higher—these are your *target areas* for improvement.

Pay close attention to these sections of this chapter, and look at the How to Make It Happen advice on strengthening each of these habits.

Table 3.1 **Self-Assessment Results**

Eat Well	Stay Hydrated	Get Enough Sleep	Exercise Regularly	Manage Stress
Question 1: A = 3 B = 2 C = 1	Question 2: A = 3 B = 2 C = 1	Question 3: A = 3 B = 2 C = 1	Question 4: A = 3 B = 2 C = 1	Question 5: A = 1 B = 2 C = 3
Question 6: A = 3 B = 2 C = 1	Question 7: A = 3 B = 2 C = 1	Question 8: A = 1 B = 2 C = 3	Question 9: A = 3 B = 2 C = 1	Question 10: A = 2 B = 1 C = 3
Question 11: A = 2 B = 3 C = 1	Question 12: A = 3 B = 2 C = 1	Question 13: A = 3 B = 1 C = 2	Question 14: A = 3 B = 2 C = 1	Question 15: A = 1 B = 2 C = 3
Total =	Total =	Total =	Total =	Total =

If you scored 5 to 6 in any category, this may also be a target area for you. Pay attention to the corresponding section in this chapter, including How to Make It Happen.

If you scored 4 or lower in any category, this area is likely an area of strength for you (Congrats!). For more ideas on how to continue excelling at this health and wellness habit, pay attention to the corresponding section of this chapter, and decide whether any of the How to Make It Happen advice would help you to strengthen this habit even more.

EAT WELL

You are what you eat from your head down to your feet.
—Pajama Sam, comic adventure character that children of the 1980s might remember

While I'm tempted to unleash a torrent of diet and nutrition research on you to explain why you should follow this rule of thumb, I've included a lot

New Alpha Rule of Thumb

Eat small meals throughout the day that include a variety of non-processed foods from the major food groups and that are sufficient to sustain your energy output.

of it in the Notes section at the end of this book, which you can peruse at your leisure. For now, I'll simply say that a healthy diet means eating the right amount of the right foods in five to six small meals throughout the day to support your daily energy expenditure.[1]

It would be lovely if there were a magic formula that all of us could follow to figure out exactly what to eat in order to look and feel our best, but the truth is that this doesn't actually exist, and instead most people will find that certain dietary tweaks (for example, less salt, more monounsaturated fats, more protein) work better or worse for them, depending on their preferences, genetics, health status, and lifestyle factors.

With that said, the suggestions below will give you a solid starting point for eating well. If you want to get super serious about optimizing your diet, consider seeing a nutritionist to find out what type of eating plan will work best for you.

New Alpha Tip

Many popular health insurance plans cover the services of a nutritionist.

How to Make It Happen

There are three main steps to eating like a champ (in other words, using food to support your nutritional and energy needs):

- Determine what to eat.

- Determine when to eat.

- Determine how much to eat, based on your energy needs.

Step 1. Determine What to Eat. The key is diversity. Basically, you want to *eat a variety of foods from the major food groups*: fruits, vegetables, whole grains, low-fat dairy products (or dairy substitutes), and lean protein, which includes lean meats, eggs, beans and legumes, nuts, seeds, and healthy fats. In selecting foods, try to *avoid any foods that are high in trans fat, cholesterol, salt (sodium), and added sugars—basically, most processed foods.* Google "DASH diet" to see example eating plans that meet these criteria, and check out "Eat Well" under Chapter 3 in *The New Alpha Resource Guide* for a few of my favorite healthy eating resources.

If eating more healthfully involves major changes in your lifestyle, try eating just one healthy meal a day differently, and see how that goes. Then, when you feel ready, aim for two healthy meals a day, and so on, depending on what's realistic and/or feasible for you. Remember, a small change that you can stick to is better than no change at all.

Step 2. Determine When to Eat. If you don't already eat five to six small meals a day, then adjusting to this approach may require taking a moment to think about *when* you'll eat. Many of us have already incorporated the standard breakfast, lunch, and dinner times into our schedule, but what happens when you also need to think about a midmorning and midafternoon snack?

My suggestion is to make these snacks super easy and low prep (like cheese sticks, nuts, fruits, and raw veggies). Just make sure that all of your meals (breakfast, lunch, dinner—plus the snacks) are roughly the same size, in terms of calories.

Step 3. Determine How Much to Eat. If you ask most "experts" how much you should be eating, most of them will recommend that you calculate your basal metabolic rate (BMR). Start with the number of calories that you'd burn if you did absolutely no activity all day, and then adjust that number based on your activity level. The problem is that this isn't super accurate, and it will change as your activity level varies.

What I recommend instead is to focus on mastering steps 1 and 2 (above) and then gradually adjusting the amount of food that you eat, depending on what you *feel* your body needs. If all else fails and you find yourself gaining weight (or unable to lose weight when you need to), try simply not eating in the three hours before you go to bed. It's surprisingly simple and effective—and may also help you to fall asleep more easily. But, by all means, do what's best for you in terms of your own health and wellness, and be sure to consult with your physician before making any major changes.

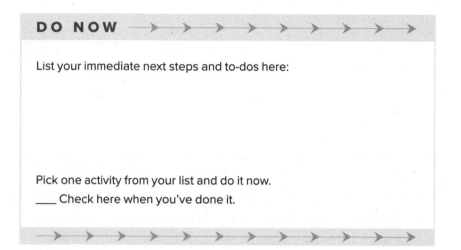

DO NOW → → → → → → → → →

List your immediate next steps and to-dos here:

Pick one activity from your list and do it now.
____ Check here when you've done it.

STAY HYDRATED

Water is the driving force of all nature.
—Leonardo da Vinci, Italian polymath and
leading Renaissance figure

New Alpha Rule of Thumb

Drink about 48 to 64 ounces of water per day.

Contrary to popular belief, there's no hard and fast rule about how much water people should drink each day. However, we do know that, in general, most healthy adults need six to eight, 8-ounce glasses of water per day—or 48 to 64 ounces total.

You might, however, need slightly more or less depending on your health, how much you exercise, and how hot or dry your climate is, so adjust your intake as necessary.

How to Make It Happen

The easiest way that I've found to make sure that I get enough water is to use a 32-ounce water bottle that I refill at least once per day. However, if you don't love the water bottle idea, you might try one of these ideas:

- Drink a glass of water first thing in the morning.

- Set the timer on your phone to go off at three-hour intervals throughout the day, and drink eight ounces of water every time it goes off.

- Force yourself to take a big drink every time you walk by a water fountain or enter a kitchen.

- Drink other fluids (not soda). Even caffeinated beverages, like coffee and tea, aren't especially dehydrating as long as you consume them in moderation.[2]

- Eat water-rich foods. These include watermelon, iceberg lettuce, celery, grapefruit, milk, yogurt, and surprisingly, even broccoli. Basically, fruits and veggies are going to be your hydration buddies.

DO NOW → → → → → → → → → →

List your immediate next steps and to-dos here:

Pick one activity from your list and do it now.
____ Check here when you've done it.

→ → → → → → → → → → →

GET ENOUGH SLEEP

*Sleep is that golden chain that ties
health and our bodies together.*
—THOMAS DEKKER, English writer

Unfortunately, we live in a world where not getting enough sleep is all too often seen as a badge of honor for high-achieving people. Most studies,

New Alpha Rule of Thumb

Aim for seven to nine hours of sleep every night.

however, suggest that adults need about seven to nine hours of sleep,[3] and depriving yourself of these critical hours (even just by a little) can significantly affect your physical and mental health, cognitive functioning, and productivity.[4]

How to Make It Happen

When I was in my twenties, I was pretty much an insomniac, and it often took me hours to fall asleep on any given night. Luckily, I got smart about sleep and developed a checklist of things to do in order to ensure that I regularly got seven to nine hours of high-quality sleep. I've reproduced this list below, so feel free to try any and all of these ideas if you're looking to improve your sleep habits:

- Try to keep a regular sleeping schedule.
- Exercise regularly, but not right before bed.
- If you like to nap during the day, don't sleep for more than 45 minutes.
- Avoid caffeine in the six hours before your bedtime.
- Avoid having more than one alcoholic drink within four hours of bedtime.
- It goes without saying, but quit smoking if you smoke—this one will help you in more ways than one!
- Avoid eating too much before bed.
- Make sure that your bed, bedding, and room temperature are comfortable.
- Don't use your bed as a workspace.
- Eliminate as much light and noise as possible. (Consider purchasing "blackout" curtains to block excess light and a sound or a white noise machine.)

- Turn off any devices that emit light (for example, cell phone, computer, or printer).

- Give yourself at least 45 minutes to wind down before going to bed.

- Write down any urgent or distracting thoughts before you go to bed. It will be easier for you to relax and fall asleep once they are on paper. I keep a notebook and pen by my bed for exactly this purpose.

- Consider a presleep ritual each night to get your mind and body prepared for sleep.

DO NOW → → → → → → → → → → →

List your immediate next steps and to-dos here:

Pick one activity from your list and do it now.
____ Check here when you've done it.

→ → → → → → → → → → → →

EXERCISE REGULARLY

Just do it!
—Nike slogan

New Alpha Rule of Thumb

Exercise daily for at least 25 minutes, include a variety of aerobic, strength training, and flexibility-focused activities, and vary your workouts.

As everyone and their mother knows, exercise provides a number of important benefits, such as these:[5]

- Protection from heart disease, stroke, certain types of cancers, type 2 diabetes, and osteoporosis

- Increased cognitive functioning later in life

- Help in falling and staying asleep

- Improved mood and increased endurance and energy levels

- Increased work productivity

- Enhanced mental ability, which helps you to build other positive habits

- Increased fitness levels and improved appearance.

In general, the U.S. Department of Health and Human services suggests that healthy adults should get 150 minutes a week of moderate aerobic activity (like swimming, walking, lawn mowing) or 75 minutes a week of vigorous aerobic activity (running, aerobic dancing) plus at least two sessions (of indeterminate length . . .) of strength training.[6] This usually amounts to about 25 minutes a day.

How to Make It Happen

1. Pick a regularly scheduled time of the day to exercise. Build a routine around exercise, so that it feels as natural a part of your day as brushing your teeth or putting your socks on. Being a strong believer in the research showing that willpower is a limited resource that decreases throughout the day,[7] I prefer to exercise early in the morning before work. My (super fit!) mom, on the other hand, swears by her evening exercise routine and regularly rewards herself with a glass of wine at the end. The key is to find the time that's most convenient for you *and* that takes advantage of your natural high-energy periods.

2. Don't obsess about finding times for your "long workout." Long workouts can be great, if that's your thing (it's not mine), but I'm honestly convinced that you don't need more than 25 minutes a day for exercise as long as you're getting your heart and respiration rates up and breaking a sweat.

Three Workout Programs That Take 25 Minutes or Less

- **Marta Montenegro Endurance Workout video.** No equipment required, three full-body progressive circuit training routines, each consisting of about 18 one-minute intervals (http://amzn.to/1YQpV9O).

- **Mark Lauren Bodyweight Training App.** No equipment required, fully customizable to your level, over 200 exercises to choose from, workouts from 2 to 40 minutes (http://apple.co/1zMy2IT).

- **The (*New York Times*–approved . . .) 7-Minute Workout.** Can be done in as little as seven minutes, requires minimal equipment (a chair and a wall), and is based on extensive research by the American College of Sports Medicine. It's also 100 percent *free* (http://apple.co/1kGQfUi).

3. Include your kids, your partner, your roommate, your friend, and/or your colleague. Some people do better at sticking with an exercise routine if they have someone to do it with. If that describes you, then grab a nearby person and invite her for a walk, run, hike, group fitness class, or frisbee date in the park.

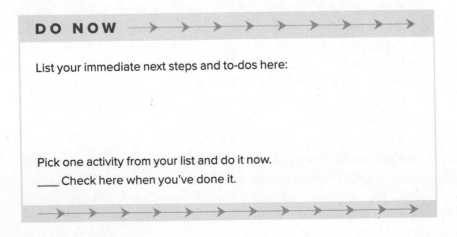

DO NOW →→→→→→→→→→→

List your immediate next steps and to-dos here:

Pick one activity from your list and do it now.
____ Check here when you've done it.

MANAGE STRESS

*To experience peace does not mean that your
life is always blissful. It means that you are capable
of tapping into a blissful state of mind amidst
the normal chaos of a hectic life.*
—Jill Bolte Taylor,
American neuroanatomist and author

New Alpha Rule of Thumb

Know how to recognize when you're stressed, and have 3 to 10 strategies that you can draw upon to productively work through (and alleviate) stress that is counterproductive.

Stress is the combination of physical, emotional, and mental responses that we experience when we are put in demanding situations—those that stretch us, challenge us, or put any sort of strain or tension on us. Examples of stress responses include increased heart rate, sweating, worrying, irritability, or mood changes.[8]

In the short run, stress can actually be a good thing—it can improve our performance and help us to quickly adapt to challenging situations. The problem, according to most researchers, is that *if it's not managed effectively, stress can actually cause or exacerbate serious health issues in the long run.*

How to Make It Happen

In my experience, effectively managing stress is a two-step process.

1. Learn to recognize the signs that you're stressed. Stress can feel different to different people. For me, it may be a feeling of nausea in the pit of my stomach. For you, it may be increased breathing and heart rate. For someone else, it might involve feeling hopeless or overwhelmed.

DO NOW

Take a moment to think about a time when you were recently stressed. How did it feel, both physically and psychologically? Take a moment to write your recollections here:

If you're having trouble identifying the physical and psychological identifiers for your stress, try talking with a close friend or family member who has been with you during multiple stressful times, and ask him what he sees when you're stressed. Ask him how you act, what kinds of things you say, and how you share what you're feeling.

2. Identify 3 to 10 ways that you can relieve stress when it starts to become counterproductive or harmful to your health. The previous sections in this chapter (eat well, stay hydrated, get enough sleep, and exercise regularly) will help you to effectively manage stress in the long run. However, there are also a handful of actions that you can take in the short term (when you are in the midst of a stressful situation) that will help you to deal with the sometimes counterproductive effects of stress.

Take a moment to think about what actions you can take "in the moment" to relieve any unproductive stress that you're feeling. These should be tailored to what *you* think will work for *you*, and they may include activities like going for a run, watching inspirational TED talks, or even having a dance party to one of your favorite songs. (Google "Hugh Grant dancing love actually" to see mine.)

DO NOW → → → → → → → → →

Jot down as many ideas as you can for short-term activities that can help you effectively manage stress:

Now, take out a sheet of paper and write down the items from the list above. Post this somewhere where you'll see it regularly and remember to use it when you need it. Figure 3.1 contains my personal list of stress busters.

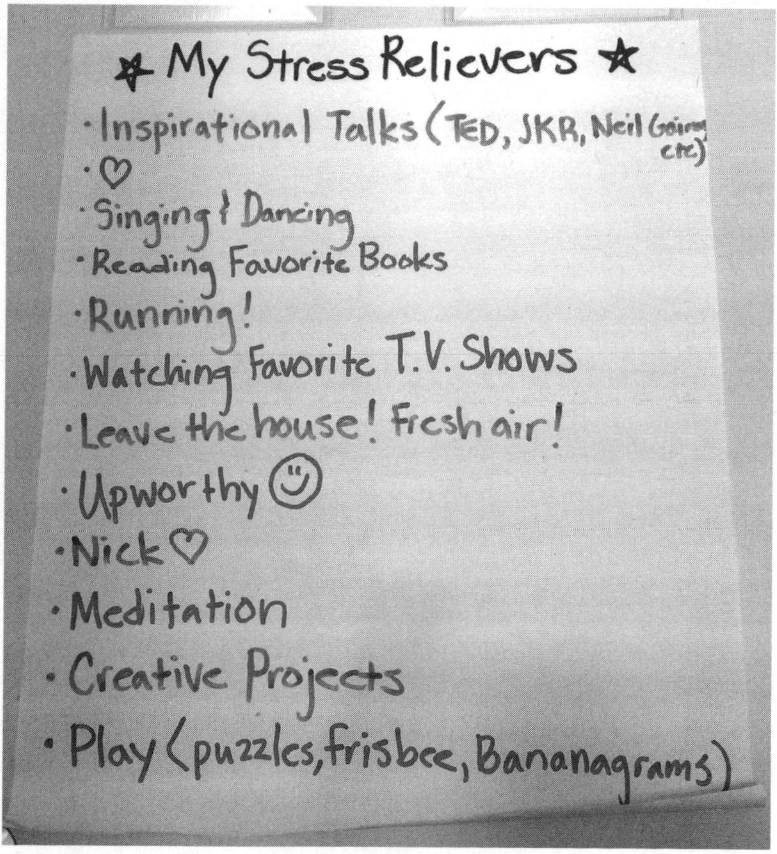

Figure 3.1 My Personal List of Stress Busters

WRAP-UP AND TRACKING PROGRESS

Step 1. Open Your *New Alpha Personal Excellence Tracker*

Open up your *New Alpha Personal Excellence Tracker* (which you down-loaded in the "Wrap-Up and Tracking Progress" section of Chapter 1).

Step 2. Customize Your Tracker

Make a list of any of the habits from this chapter that you would like to fo-cus on. These can be the exact ones discussed in this chapter or others that you came up with on your own. Write these down here:

Next, adjust the "Prioritize Your Health and Wellness" columns of the *New Alpha Personal Excellence Tracker* (these are the yellow columns) to reflect the habits that you've identified. (Note that five habits discussed in this chapter are already included, but you should edit, delete, or add to these to make them specific to your goals and needs.)

Step 3. Plan for Success

In the first column of the following chart, write out each of the health and wellness habits that you want to focus on, giving yourself a few lines of space in between each one.

In the second column, write out any obstacles that may make it diffi-cult for you to embody this habit (for example, "I have a hard time getting to bed by 11 p.m., which makes it hard to get eight hours of sleep").

In the third column, write out how you will overcome each of these obstacles (for example, "I will set a daily alarm for 9:30 p.m. to remind me to get ready for bed").

Health and Wellness Habits That I Want to Focus On	Potential Obstacles That I May Face	How I Will Overcome These Obstacles

Step 4. Track Your Progress

Continue to *update your tracker every day*. As always, do what you need to do in order to customize this process to best fit your needs.

Step 5. Follow up and Continuously Improve

Continue to review your tracker weekly. Examine the data in your tracker for the past week, and use a notebook to write down any changes that you plan to make in order to increase the likelihood of your accomplishing your goals.

Also, be sure to note progress that you've made on the habits from the previous two chapters, and don't be afraid to give yourself a high five or do a one-minute victory dance—whatever you need to do to keep yourself energized and motivated.

Develop a Mindset for Success

Attitude is a little thing that makes a big difference.
—WINSTON CHURCHILL,
British statesperson and U.K. Prime Minister

Patrick Wu is one of the most successful human beings I've ever met—and I mean successful in every sense of the word: high achieving, impactful, and fulfillment focused. As an educational advisor for the Jack Kent Cooke Foundation, Patrick provides academic advising and access to educational opportunities to the foundation's Young Scholars. Before joining the foundation, he was a public school teacher and the academic dean for the Civic Leadership Institute, a service-based summer program in partnership with Johns Hopkins University's Center for Talented Youth and Northwestern University's Center for Talent Development. In addition, Patrick is a trained challenge course facilitator, and he has led over a dozen national and international service learning and leadership trips for students from all over the world.

Patrick and I met in college. I was intrigued by his passion and seemingly endless energy and enthusiasm for his life and work (and the fact that he's a totally inspiring person to be around), so I've kept in touch with him in the years since. (See the section "Seeking out and Maintaining Relationships with High-Quality People" in Chapter 2, "Build Positive and Productive Relationships with Others.") Indeed, he has a lot of great qualities, but if I had to pinpoint the most important factor driving his success,

I'd say that it's his mindset, or the mental habits that he uses to drive positive outcomes.

Based on my experience working with people like Patrick and a few of the exciting findings from recent social science research, the ideas and activities in this chapter will help you to develop a mindset for success.

SELF-ASSESSMENT

In order to make this chapter as useful as possible for yourself, use this quick self-assessment to gauge your performance on the various aspects of mindset. Then skip ahead to the sections of this chapter that focus on the areas that you want to grow and/or develop.

To what degree do each of the following statements describe you?

1. I don't wait for others to initiate change. I take ownership of problems and figure out what needs to be done and how to do it. I follow up when necessary.

   A. This describes me very well.

   B. This describes me somewhat.

   C. This does not describe me.

2. I'm self-assured and believe in my ability to tackle any challenges that come my way. I'm hopeful about the future, and in general, I believe that things will work out.

   A. This describes me very well.

   B. This describes me somewhat.

   C. This does not describe me.

3. I feel energetic and enthusiastic about my life and work.

   A. This describes me very well.

   B. This describes me somewhat.

   C. This does not describe me.

4. I am passionate about my long-term goals, and I will work through any and all obstacles to achieve them.

   A. This describes me very well.

   B. This describes me somewhat.

   C. This does not describe me.

5. I am easily able to change course in order to respond to unexpected changes or new challenges that may come up.

   A. This describes me very well.

   B. This describes me somewhat.

   C. This does not describe me.

6. When I'm interested in a topic or issue, I am eager to learn as much as I can about it, and I ask a lot of questions.

   A. This describes me very well.

   B. This describes me somewhat.

   C. This does not describe me.

7. I'm imaginative, and I frequently think about new ideas and/or better ways of doing things.

   A. This describes me very well.

   B. This describes me somewhat.

   C. This does not describe me.

8. I regularly take time to reflect on what I'm grateful for and to thank and appreciate others.

   A. This describes me very well.

   B. This describes me somewhat.

   C. This does not describe me.

9. I can laugh at myself or find humor in otherwise challenging situations.

   A. This describes me very well.

   B. This describes me somewhat.

   C. This does not describe me.

10. I view failure as a necessary component of progress, and I use my failures as learning experiences.

    A. This describes me very well.

    B. This describes me somewhat.

    C. This does not describe me.

In the chart below:

1. Put an *X* in column A for each question above that you answered A—these are your probable *areas of strength* around mindset.

2. Put an *X* in column C for each question that you answered C—these will be your *primary areas of focus* for this chapter.

3. Put an *X* in column B for each question that you answered B—these are your *secondary areas of focus* around mindset. They're important, but not as important as your main areas of focus.

My Answer	A (Area of Strength)	B (Secondary Focus)	C (Primary Focus)
Question 1. Be Proactive	____	____	____
Question 2. Be Confident and Optimistic	____	____	____
Question 3. Cultivate Zest	____	____	____
Question 4. Develop Grit	____	____	____
Question 5. Be Adaptable	____	____	____
Question 6. Be Curious	____	____	____
Question 7. Think Creatively	____	____	____

My Answer	A (Area of Strength)	B (Secondary Focus)	C (Primary Focus)
Question 8. Practice Gratitude	____	____	____
Question 9. Have a Sense of Humor	____	____	____
Question 10. Embrace Failure and Continuous Improvement	____	____	____

BE PROACTIVE

If in charge, take charge; in the absence of policy, create your own; when everyone else is standing still, move out.
—Variously attributed

When I was promoted to the chief of operations role at the Carnegie Foundation, all everyone kept asking me immediately after it was announced was, "How did you get that job?!?"—and I'll admit, at age 30, I was absolutely younger and less experienced than the rest of the organization's senior leadership team. But the job didn't just fall into my lap in a stroke of luck or happenstance, and I certainly didn't (and still don't, unfortunately . . .) possess some magical quality that inexplicably made good things like this happen to me.

In actuality, the job didn't exist immediately before I filled it. I got it because I told the president, Tony Bryk, "I think we need a chief of operations, and I think I'm the person to fill the role," to which he responded, "I've been thinking the exact same thing." I mean, sure, I'd worked my tail off for the organization and had done the research to show *why* we needed this role and *why* I thought I was the person to fill it, but in essence, I got the job because I asked for it. I honestly have no idea whether I would have been offered the job if I hadn't asked.

The point is that being proactive is all about not waiting for others to initiate change. It's about recognizing what's needed and then taking the initiative and making it happen. Whether this involves making a case for what you want or identifying a problem and taking the lead to find a solution, I can tell you, as someone who's been in supervisory positions and in supervisee positions, that leaders and managers *love* this quality. It makes their lives infinitely easier when they know they have someone on their team whom they can trust to get just about anything done, no matter how initially challenging, vague, or ambiguous. It also means that proactive people are almost always at the top of their supervisors' mind when it comes to promotions and special projects.

Sure, there's a certain risk to being proactive—namely, that you might step on someone's toes. And, yes, this does happen from time to time, but if I look at all the times that my being proactive resulted in someone else's getting pissed off at my initiative, those instances are few and far between compared to the situations in which being proactive resulted in pure awesomeness (like getting a promotion). As I learned from my fellow Silicon Valley nerds, "Don't ask for permission. Ask for forgiveness." This advice was life changing.

One last point on being proactive: successfully implementing this aspect of mindset also entails following up with people. This includes the people you work with (whether you supervise them, they supervise you, or you're just working on a project together), and the people you meet.

For instance, if you meet a superstar at some networking event, *you* should follow up within 24 hours (while the social momentum is still hot and she remembers who you are!). It's amazing how many people I meet, who profess to be in love with the work that I do, but then either never follow up after we meet or follow up weeks or months later when I have no recollection of who they are. Those who follow up within 24 hours definitely get noticed and often also get my time and attention—if only because it signals something rare and special about them and makes me think they'd be easy and delightful people to know and work with. Think about it: if you're a busy professional, and you have 50 or more people reaching out to you a month who are all trying to get your time and attention, wouldn't you be more likely to follow up with the one who was quick and enthusiastic and who made it easy to help them?

Also, don't be afraid to follow up again in another week if you haven't received a response—people get busy, and as my partner and fiancé, Nick, reminded me recently: "Never underestimate the power of that second annoying email." Feel free to politely (and graciously!) follow up until the recipient responds or gives you a firm no to your request. Keep in mind that I've never actually had the latter happen, but I have followed up with people multiple times if I really, really wanted to connect with them, and it's always paid off.

How to Make It Happen

- Think about someone whom you've recently met, and whom you want to develop a relationship with. Send him an email and invite him for coffee—which you should pay for.

- Tell your boss that you're interested in a promotion, and ask what you need to accomplish in order to get there. One of the worst and most annoying things that I see people doing now more than ever is to assume that they automatically deserve a promotion simply because they want one and have asked for one. Rather than looking proactive and confident, this comes across as annoying and arrogant (especially from someone who thinks she's proven herself but has not). It is, however, perfectly okay (and even good) to graciously express interest in taking on more and bigger challenges in your role and to ask what is necessary in order to advance to the next role. Then humbly work your tail off to get there.

- Share an idea that you have with the group. If you have a great idea, figure out the right channel (your boss, an email, a group meeting), and put it out there.

- Interested in exploring an alternative career? Get the ball rolling by signing up for some volunteer work in that area. (For ideas here, see "Kindness and Generosity" under Chapter 1 in *The New Alpha Resource Guide*.)

- Point out a potential problem that you see, *and* have a solution ready. Nothing frustrates colleagues and team members faster than a person who insists on poking holes in everything but has no good solutions to address the problems that he is pointing out.

- When you're handed a tough project or task, ask the person who's giving it to you to define the "vision for success"—or to name three things that need to be true in order for this assignment to be considered "successfully completed."

- Interested in working on a particular project with someone? Ask her how you can help (even if it's not in your job description). Bonus points if you're just helpful for the sake of being helpful.

- See a problem in your organization that no one is tackling? Identify three ways that you can make a difference, and take action!

DO NOW → → → → → → → → → →

List your immediate next steps and to-dos here:

Pick one activity from your list and do it now.
____ Check here when you've done it.

→ → → → → → → → → → → →

BE CONFIDENT AND OPTIMISTIC

Optimism is the faith that leads to achievement.
Nothing can be done without hope and confidence.
—HELEN KELLER, American author,
political activist, and lecturer; first person who was deaf
and blind to earn a bachelor of arts degree

When Melanie Gleason started Attorney on the Move (www.attorneyon themove.com), a nonprofit virtual law office that provides pro bono law services to members of historically underserved communities, she was creating a model of legal support and representation that had never been done before. Many of her friends and colleagues warned her that launching this idea would be risky, if not impossible, but Melanie had a passion for this project, confidence that she had the necessary legal and coaching skills to bring this project to life, and a belief that it was possible. So she quit her day job, launched a crowd-funding campaign, packed everything she owned into a Smart car, and hit the road. At the time of this writing, she has raised over $30,000 from people all over the world to bring Attorney on the Move to life.

Confidence is all about having self-assurance and belief in your abilities—especially when you're facing an unknown or particularly difficult challenge, like taking on a new role, leading a new project in your organization, or—as in Melanie's case—launching an entirely new organization. Similarly, *optimism* means being hopeful about the future and believing that things will work out. Being confident and optimistic doesn't mean being arrogant (an exaggerated sense of your own abilities) or oblivious of the challenges that may lie ahead. Rather, this aspect of mindset entails doing what you can to understand the situation, making sure that you have a realistic plan to tackle any challenges that may lie ahead (including calling on others for help when necessary), and believing in your ability to be successful with hard work and persistence.

How to Make It Happen

- One thing that Casey Gerald (see the "Develop Grit" section of this chapter) shared with me is that just before he gave his now-famous Harvard Class Day speech, his grandmother reminded him to *get out of his own way* so that the message could get out. In other words, if we take our ego out of a situation and we see ourselves as the *vessel* for a message or outcome that's bigger than ourselves, it makes it a lot easier to do whatever it is that we need to do in order to move forward.

- Fake it till you make it. Some people hate this advice, but I swear it works. If you find yourself in a situation in which you feel that you're in over your head when it comes to your abilities, just act *as if* you don't feel that way. For instance, I often do this before I have to give a big talk or presentation. Over time, you won't need to fake it. It'll start to feel natural. Keep in mind that this doesn't mean that you should avoid asking for advice or help when you need it. Rather, it means recognizing that it's okay to feel scared and overwhelmed when you're taking on something really big and really new—but then doing it anyway.

- Practice, practice, practice. Whether giving speeches, having difficult conversations, or asking for a raise, these types of activities always go better if you've thought about what you want to say and you have practiced actually saying it out loud beforehand. Also, don't be afraid to have a few notes handy.

- Have a personal affirmation that you repeat to yourself before nerve-racking events. Author and leadership coach Achim Nowak suggests: "I am a vibrant vehicle of light and love." Whatever affirmation you come up with, it should be confidence boosting *and* make you feel good. (You might use your *Personal Leadership Identity Statement*, which we'll talk about more in Chapter 6.)

- When taking on a big challenge, envision the ideal outcome. What does it look like? How do you feel? Now think of at least three big obstacles that you may need to overcome to get there. How will you get around these challenges? Be as specific as possible here.

- Pretend to be your future self 10 years down the road. Write a letter to your current self that encourages you to take on big challenges or risks that have the potential to change your life.

- Ask a mentor or someone you respect to share his strategies for believing in himself and staying positive in difficult circumstances.

- Ask someone you love or trust to share what she thinks are your three best qualities. Post these somewhere you can look at them regularly, and remind yourself of them when you need a boost.

DO NOW → → → → → → → → →

List your immediate next steps and to-dos here.

Pick one activity from your list and do it now.
___ Check here when you've done it.

CULTIVATE ZEST

*Zest is the secret of all beauty. There is no beauty that is
attractive without zest.*
—CHRISTIAN DIOR, French fashion designer

When I first met Andrew Motiwalla, founder and chairperson at Terra Education, he burst through the doors of the downtown Palo Alto coffee shop where we were scheduled to meet in a whirlwind of excitement and energy and announced, "It's great to meet you! Kermit [our mutual friend] told me so much about you. I can't wait to hear more and tell you about our program—after I grab a cup of hot chocolate!"

When he returned with his drink, we talked all about my history and experiences as a teacher, and he shared with me a bit more about his program, which was an international leadership and service learning organization for teens, and what they were working on—including how I might fit in. By the end of the meeting, I was inspired by Andrew's boundless passion and enthusiasm, and I quickly signed up for one of the lowest-paying (and most awesome!) jobs of my life. I figured that even if the job were horrible, it would be a blast working with Andrew. Turned out that the job was incredible (I worked with the organization for three summers in South Africa, Brazil, and Costa Rica), and nine years later, Andrew is still one of the most fun and motivational leaders I know.

Put simply, Andrew has *zest*—enthusiasm and excitement for life and all that he does, and this makes it very, very enjoyable to work with him. No matter what the situation, he's always energetically and passionately pushing the work forward. The best part about Andrew is that he's not faking it—he genuinely loves what he does, and it shows.

How to Make It Happen

- Consider this: what three things do you need in order to feel energized and excited in your daily life? How can you bring these things to your work, your free time, or your daily routines? For instance, I need to be around awesome people, so I make a point to have regular meetings with people who inspire and motivate me and to partner with clients whose work I deeply believe in. Use the space below to jot down a few quick ideas for what makes you feel energized and excited in your work. How can you incorporate this into your current role?

- Get enough sleep. (See Chapter 3, "Prioritize Your Health and Wellness.") It's much easier to be zesty when you've had enough resty . . .

- Shout out "Yes!" or give "snaps" the next time you're listening to a speaker with whom you agree. Bonus points if you shout out "Woot." This can be an in-person type of deal (for example, at a conference), or it can be directed at just your computer screen.

- Pick a "get pumped" theme song that you can play when you need an extra energy or enthusiasm boost. (My standby here is "Jump" by The Pointer Sisters.)

DO NOW → → → → → → → → →

List your immediate next steps and to-dos here:

Pick one activity from your list and do it now.
____ Check here when you've done it.

DEVELOP GRIT

Do. Or do not. There is no try.
—YODA, legendary Jedi Master

Casey Gerald is one of the most extraordinary and inspiring people I've ever interviewed. Abandoned by both of his parents as a child and raised by relatives, friends, and his older sister, he's survived everything from being robbed at gunpoint to working at Lehman Brothers during the financial crisis in 2008. A Yale graduate with a Harvard MBA, Casey gave the Harvard Class Day speech in 2014, which has since gone viral. (Google "Casey Gerald Harvard Class Day" for your daily dose of inspiration and hope for humanity.) He also recently gave a TED talk and previously co-founded MBAxAmerica, in order to support economic and community growth by connecting MBA students from top business schools with entrepreneurs across the country.

When I asked Casey what aspect of his personality got him where he is today, he answered this way:

> High tolerance for suffering—one of the things that bothers me about the conversation that people have about following your dreams, passion, and so on, is that often the people who are saying it are the people who don't have much at stake. They don't have to worry too much about bills, or they have connections, trust funds, and so on. But the reality is that life is really freaking hard. Besides the material needs, we have emotional, psychological, physical, etc., needs as well, so I'm never flippant about what's at stake. When someone says I'm going to pursue my dream, or passion, or purpose, that's very serious business, and in many ways, the world conspires to fight against you. I wish we had a healthier dialogue about suffering—so that we could be honest about it, and so that people who are suffering don't feel like it's the end or [that they're abnormal for some reason].

Similarly, my partner and fiancé, Nick Warren, once told me this:

If you're doing anything really meaningful or that in any way challenges the status quo, it will absolutely bring you to your knees at one point or another—but if you can get through that, if you can just force yourself to be okay with failure and the unknown—and keep going, then you can do incredible things in your life and in the world.

Researchers have a name for what Casey and Nick describe as the ability to endure incredible hardship and continue persisting toward long-term goals: *grit*. More than just being passionate, being gritty is about keeping your eye on the prize and persisting in the face of seemingly endless challenges and obstacles.[1]

How to Make It Happen

- What are you passionate about in this world? What one thing do you most want to accomplish in life? What steps do you need to take in order to do this? Jot down your ideas here:

  What one step can you take *right now*? Do it.

- I'm convinced that grit can start small with basic activities that we feel unmotivated to do. What task do you most dread that's on your plate right now (for example, emptying the cat litter box, washing your dishes, doing laundry, cleaning your bathroom, or drafting the budget for a work project)? Set a timer for 10, 15, or 20 minutes, and do as much of this task as you can. You're free to quit when the timer goes off. If necessary, call a friend and ask him to call you back in 10, 15, or 20 minutes to check on your progress.

- Make yourself accountable to someone: commit to your boss, partner, roommate, or someone else that you will accomplish a specific task by a specific date. It helps if this is someone whom you actually want to impress.

- Write a letter to yourself, and describe the three best aspects of your personality or character that will allow you to be successful at the task that you most dread (for example, "I'm hardworking, I'm thoughtful, and I pay attention to the details"), and explain how you will use these strengths to get the job done.

DO NOW → → → → → → → → → →

List your immediate next steps and to-dos here:

Pick one activity from your list and do it now.
___ Check here when you've done it.

→ → → → → → → → → → → → →

BE ADAPTABLE

The willow is my favorite tree. I grew up near one. It's the most flexible tree in nature, and nothing can break it—no wind, no elements. It can bend and withstand anything.
—Pink, American singer-songwriter

One of my all-time favorite colleagues is Nisha Patel. Nisha currently manages the corporate and foundation relations for Global Citizen Year, an international nonprofit that recruits and trains high-potential graduating seniors out of high school and places them in projects in Africa, Latin America, and Asia during a bridge year before college. I met her when we were both working at the Carnegie Foundation. During our time as colleagues, Nisha was always calm, cool, and collected (and even enthusiastic) in high-stress situations. When last-minute changes came down the pipeline, she had no trouble immediately shifting gears. In these cases, you'd often hear her say things like, "Oh, we're overhauling the entire organization's project management system, and it needs to be done by tomorrow? Okay, let's get started!" or "Next Friday's meeting with out-of-state partners has been moved up to this Friday, and everyone needs new airline and hotel reservations? Okay, I'll start contacting people!"

No matter what the situation, or how late in the game it was, Nisha was always totally *adaptable*. She responded flexibly to unexpected changes and new challenges, and she was able to change course when necessary. Relatedly, she was quick on her feet and could easily see the connections between any necessary changes and the current projects—an ability that greatly helped to minimize interruptions to the workflow. Because of this, everyone wanted to work with her, and everyone was thrilled when she was promoted to a project management position in the organization, a role that she naturally excelled at.

How to Make It Happen

- Take a different route to work tomorrow. Let the stress of a broken routine wash over you like a hot river of awesomeness.

- The next time your boss changes her plans at the last minute or asks you to change directions on a project, name three reasons why this change could be good. If you have the opportunity, tell her what these reasons are.

- Mix up one of your daily routines. For instance, if you normally run or swim, take a group exercise class instead. If you normally drink coffee, try chai tea or another new beverage.

- Under what circumstances are you the least flexible? Why is this? Is there anything that you can do or change to be more adaptable when these situations arise?

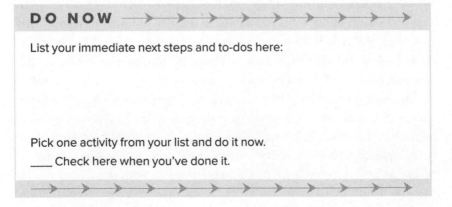

DO NOW

List your immediate next steps and to-dos here:

Pick one activity from your list and do it now.
____ Check here when you've done it.

BE CURIOUS

Look up at the stars and not down at your feet.
Try to make sense of what you see, and wonder about
what makes the universe exist. Be curious.
—STEPHEN HAWKING, English theoretical physicist,
cosmologist, and author

Growing up in Chicago, my friend Sarah Anzia became interested in local politics. She was always curious about who votes when and how this affects the outcomes of elections. If all the teachers' union supporters come out to vote in a single election, can that swing an election? Sarah was nothing if not curious. Her curiosity eventually led her to the University of Chicago, where she got a master's in public policy, and later to Stanford, where she researched this issue even further, as a PhD student. Now an assistant professor at UC Berkeley, Sarah is a nationally recognized expert on interest groups and local elections.

She gained this recognition because she found a topic that interested and excited her, and then she spent years exploring, studying, and asking questions until she found the answers she was looking for. Now, I'm not saying you have to go get a PhD as Sarah did, but I am saying that if you're really interested in something, it's worth exploring in depth and seeing where it takes you. At best, you'll become a recognized expert, and at worst, you'll learn something new, which is still a pretty good outcome.

Also, don't forget to ask questions! Early on in my career, I worried that if I asked too many questions, I might seem incompetent or as if I shouldn't be in the room. But, over time, I realized that the people in the room who were asking questions were often the best critical thinkers— they were curious about and engaged in whatever was being discussed. What's more, I'm convinced that the only reason we're taught to shut up and listen is because this makes it easy for people in power to avoid being challenged, which is total B.S. If you're curious about something, do what you need to do in order to get the answer. Whether that involves conducting research, asking people questions, reading everything you can get your hands on—just do it. The most intelligent, interesting, and insightful people I know are the curious ones.

How to Make It Happen

- Google the "best nonfiction books" in a category that you're interested in but that has nothing to do with your area of expertise. Pick one and buy it or check it out from your local library and read it. If you like it, try another one.

- The next time someone asks you to do something that doesn't quite make sense to you, say, "Okay, this sounds interesting. Just to make sure we're on the same page, can you please explain why we're doing X instead of Y?" (where X is the new instruction and Y is what you'd do otherwise).

- The next time someone asks you a question that you don't know the answer to, go look it up. Don't stop until you have an answer. Revel in the delight that comes from seeking and finding the answer to a hard question.

- Go to your local bookstore or library. Find a section that you normally wouldn't go to, and pick out a book that looks interesting to skim. Now, pick the least interesting book you can find, and give it a skim as well.

- What activity have you always been interested in but never done? If possible, do this activity now, or make an appointment to do it (for example, swinging on a trapeze, hang-gliding, exploring the Great Wall of China, or running a 10K).

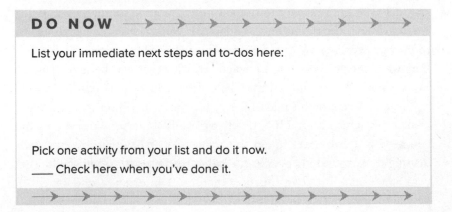

DO NOW

List your immediate next steps and to-dos here:

Pick one activity from your list and do it now.
____ Check here when you've done it.

THINK CREATIVELY

*Creativity is putting your imagination to work, and it's
produced the most extraordinary results in human culture.*
—SIR KEN ROBINSON, English speaker,
author, and educational advisor

"Let's write a song about quality improvement and teach it to everyone!" shouted Nicole Gray and Rachel Mudge in unison. Nicole and Rachel are math professors at Foothill College in Los Altos, California, and both helped to launch the community college math program at the Carnegie Foundation. They also both happen to be the kind of people who are always thinking creatively—that is, coming up with original and imaginative ideas for how to make things work.

In this particular case, we were at a staff retreat and trying to figure out how to get the entire foundation staff—everyone from program teams to the operations folks to the public relations department—to understand and get excited about quality improvement, which was a key part of our work. Rather than give a PowerPoint lecture on the topic or having everyone read and discuss a book or handout, with Nicole and Rachel in the lead (which was critical since my own musical ability is embarrassingly low . . .), we created a song about it. The song was a success in terms of helping people to better understand our work, *and* it forced us to really hone in on the main ideas since it was not an especially long song. Even years later, if someone happened to whistle that tune, a handful of people would start singing the improvement song. That, my friend, is thinking creatively, and according to a recent survey of over 1,500 global CEOs, it's the most important factor required for long-term success in an increasingly complex world.[2]

How to Make It Happen

- Read poetry. In my opinion, poetry is one of the most important and underrated tools in our leadership arsenal. Think about it: it forces you to turn on your intuition and start making connections between things, which is something that highly effective leaders need to be able to do, *and* it often draws on your emotions (which builds *emotional intelligence*). Personally, I recommend Lucille Clifton, Dylan Thomas, and Mary Oliver, but make a trip to your local bookstore or library and see what intrigues you.

- Get outside of your home or workplace, and take 20 pictures of things that you think are beautiful.

- Go to Reddit.com's *Writing Prompts* subreddit and answer one of them. Post your answer on Reddit.

- Think of two things that you enjoy, and imagine what they would be like if you put them together. Put them together and see what happens. For instance, I like hiking and science fiction. So, I could write a sci-fi short story with a plot that involves hiking.

- Step away from your work for 10 to 15 minutes, and do something that's fun and entirely unrelated to your work like working on a jigsaw puzzle or playing with Play-Doh or having a conversation with your colleague about what he did last weekend. Often, taking time and space away from a project will reenergize your creative perspective.

DO NOW → → → → → → → → → → →

List your immediate next steps and to-dos here:

Pick one activity from your list and do it now.
____ Check here when you've done it.

PRACTICE GRATITUDE

Gratitude is the sign of noble souls.
—AESOP, ancient Greek
(and possibly fictitious) storyteller(s)

Patrick Smith is a friend of mine from college who recently took a job in Spain. Instead of reveling in the awesome culture, great food, and outstanding sites, when he arrived in Spain, he quite unexpectedly found himself homesick, overworked, and frustrated with the language barrier. After hearing him complain about it for several weeks, another friend gently suggested that he think of three Spain-specific things that he was grateful for each day. He's been posting them on Facebook, and it's a blast to follow. Among other things, he's written about Spanish pride, street art, and Tinto de Verano.

Patrick ended his "gratitude project" a few days ago and posted this message: "I know I will continue to have great and horrible days, but at least now I know a way to combat the negativity, and I'll think or recall all the great things I've already seen and learned about Spain. I've also been able to *accept* those differences that made me upset. If you are in a negative space right now, I highly recommend you do this exercise. Just two weeks of this made a huge change in the perspective I had on Spain." Patrick's experience isn't surprising since research shows that the number one mindset factor that affects our long-term fulfillment is gratitude.[3]

How to Make It Happen

- Think about three things that you're grateful for, and write them down here:

- Make or buy a beautiful book in which to write down three things that you're grateful for every day.

- Think of someone who's helped you recently. Write her a quick note or email to say thanks.

- Think of someone who helped you as a child. Write him a quick note or email to say thanks. I did this with my favorite childhood teacher, and that's why we've kept in touch for almost 30 years.

- Wave enthusiastically to someone who lets you cut into her lane during busy traffic.

- If you run into your postal delivery person, thank him!

- Thank the grocery store clerk who rings you up.

- Tell your parents or caregivers what you're most grateful for about how they raised you. (As is typical of we millennials, I do this to my parents all the time—I'm pretty sure they think I'm weird, but they love it nonetheless.)

- Tell your partner or best friends three reasons why you're grateful for their presence in your life.

- Write down the three aspects of your personality or skills that you're most grateful for.

- Write down three hard life lessons that you're most grateful for.

DO NOW → → → → → → → → →

List your immediate next steps and to-dos here:

Pick one activity from your list and do it now.
____ Check here when you've done it.

HAVE A SENSE OF HUMOR

The most wasted of all days is one without laughter.
—E. E. CUMMINGS, American poet,
painter, essayist, author, and playwright

"Um . . . these look like penguins and not seals," I whispered to my colleague and supervisor, Annabel Smith. At that exact moment, we were about halfway through a multihour (and somewhat nausea-inducing) boat tour with a group of high school students off the coast of Cape Town, South Africa.

After many days of being cooped up inside our dormitory building due to heavy rains, we'd promised the students that we were going to tour a glorious island of seals, but due to a mix-up we found ourselves staring at an entire island of—not seals but penguins. "Do you think they'll notice?" Annabel deadpanned. I looked at her confused for a moment, and then we both burst out laughing.

Of course, despite my overanxious worrying, none of the students seemed too concerned that "Seal Island" was filled with penguins, and I learned a valuable lesson that day: having a sense of humor or being able to laugh at yourself or find humor in otherwise challenging situations makes everything more fun (and memorable). When you're a leader, people look to you for how to react. If they see that you can roll with the punches and even laugh at yourself, they'll roll right along with you. If they see you freak out (and this is especially true with teenagers), they will eat you alive.

How to Make It Happen

- Think about what makes you laugh. Are there certain people, types of movies, particular memes, or kinds of situations that make you laugh? Make an effort to put yourself in situations in which you are exposed to people and things that make you laugh.

- Watch a funny movie. For me, there is nothing funnier than the movie *Stepbrothers*. I laugh so hard every time I watch it, and because of it, whenever I'm in a big space with other people, I can't help but quote Will Ferrel: "So much space for activities!"

- Have at least one friend or family member with whom you can be silly. For me, my partner, Nick, is generally a very serious and fairly contained person, but he has this hilarious sense of humor that he'll only use when we're alone. Once when we were playing a very competitive game of Bananagrams and it was clear that I was about to win, I said in a kind of evil, Ursula-like voice, "You're mine!" to which he responded, "I don't like this . . . I'm starting to feel like the Little Mermaid." It still makes me laugh to think about it.

- Read books by comedians. I love Tina Fey's *Bossypants* and anything by David Sedaris or Augusten Burroughs.

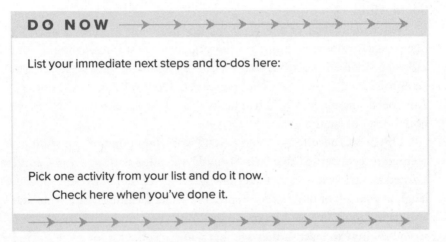

DO NOW → → → → → → → → → →

List your immediate next steps and to-dos here:

Pick one activity from your list and do it now.
____ Check here when you've done it.

EMBRACE FAILURE AND CONTINUOUS IMPROVEMENT

I hope that in this year to come, you make mistakes. Because if you are making mistakes, then you are making new things, trying new things, learning, living, pushing yourself, changing yourself, changing your world. You're doing things you've never done before, and more importantly, you're doing something.
—NEIL GAIMAN, English author

All of the most successful (and depending where they are in the process, most fulfilled) people I know have experienced some major failure somewhere along the way to where they are now. Take my friend Ellen Cassidy, for example. Ellen is a wildly successful private LSAT tutor, who's found success doing work that she loves. However, in her words, "I've been rejected from every full-time job I've ever applied to. I did my American Conservatory Theater (ACT) fellowship because I got rejected from Google. I dropped out of my MFA program after one semester. I was waitlisted at Stanford Law, and I had the slot just below the last person they admitted. And yet, all of this gave me the opportunity to take the risk I needed to find my true passion and make the difference I needed to make. I wouldn't trade all that for the world."

Whether you experience failure in your life or your career (or both, you lucky duck!), the truth is that as you achieve bigger and bigger things, you're going to encounter more and more risk, and thus, more failure. I'm sorry to be the one to tell you this, but that's just how life works. Some people never really get comfortable with this reality, and so they stop growing and taking chances. But, assuming that you do want to keep moving forward, then you're going to have to make friends with failure and learn to use the experience as a tool to understand what works and what doesn't under different types of conditions.

How to Make It Happen

- Put yourself in uncomfortable situations as early and as often as you can. You'll mess up, but you'll get comfortable with not being perfect, and you'll learn quickly how to get better. Honestly, the people whom I feel most sorry for are those incredibly high achieving people who've never failed at anything; it must be lonely and paralyzing up there on that perfect pedestal. They're never able to do what they really want to do because they are terrified by the prospect of messing up. Instead, we imperfectionists mess up all the time, and while this often feels absolutely terrifying, it also feels liberating and empowering. Onward and upward!

- Think of a recent failure that you've had (or the most recent one that you can remember). Name three reasons why you're grateful for that failure, including what you learned from it. What will you do differently next time?

- Think of three famous people whom you respect and/or admire. Now Google them, and identify at least one major failure that each of them experienced. Write down your findings here:

- Keep a *celebrations board*—a place where you write down goals that you've achieved or positive accomplishments in your life. When you're feeling down about a failure, use the celebrations board to help keep things in perspective.

- Keep a *failures board*—on the left side of the board, write down each failure or setback that you experience. On the right side of the board, write down what you learned from this experience and what you'll do differently next time.

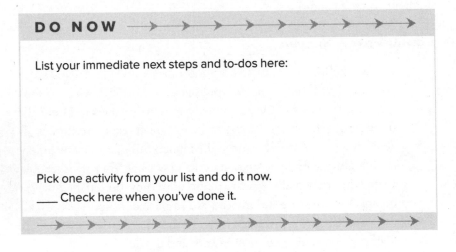

DO NOW →→→→→→→→→→

List your immediate next steps and to-dos here:

Pick one activity from your list and do it now.
____ Check here when you've done it.

WRAP-UP AND TRACKING PROGRESS

Step 1. Open Your *New Alpha Personal Excellence Tracker*

Open up your *New Alpha Personal Excellence Tracker* (which you downloaded in the "Wrap-Up and Tracking Progress" section of Chapter 1).

Step 2. Customize Your Tracker

Make a list of any of the mental habits from this chapter that you would like to focus on in your personal and/or professional life. These can be from the specific habits covered in this chapter or others that you came up with on your own. Write these down here:

Next, adjust the "Develop a Mindset for Success" columns of the *New Alpha Personal Excellence Tracker* (these are the green columns) to reflect the specific habits that you've identified. (Note that the habits outlined in this chapter are already included, but you should edit, delete, or add to these to make them specific to your goals and/or needs.)

Step 3. Plan for Success

In the first column of the chart below, write out each habit from this chapter that you want to focus on, giving yourself a few lines of space in between each one. In the second column, write out any obstacles that may hinder you from adopting a particular habit (for example, "I have a hard time remembering to practice gratitude"). In the third column, write out how you will overcome each of these obstacles (for example, "I will set an alarm on my phone for 5 p.m. each day to remind me to write down three things that I'm grateful for").

Mindset for Success Habits That I Want to Focus On	Potential Obstacles That I May Face	How I Will Overcome These Obstacles

Step 4. Track Your Progress

Continue to *update your tracker every day*. As always, do what you need to do in order to customize this process to best fit your needs.

Step 5. Follow up and Continuously Improve

Continue to review your tracker weekly. Examine the data in your tracker for the past week, and use a notebook to write down any changes that you plan to make in order to increase your likelihood of accomplishing your goals. Don't forget to recognize and celebrate progress that you've made on habits from previous chapters.

CHAPTER

5

Psychological and Organizational Strategies to Help You Achieve Your Goals

You must do the thing you think you cannot do.
—ELEANOR ROOSEVELT, American politician,
diplomat, and activist

Wouldn't it be nice if we were all built with extraordinarily high levels of internal motivation, energy, and competence, so that we could accomplish anything and everything that we truly wanted to do? By now, you're nearly finished with Part I of this program, "Personal Excellence," and (assuming you don't have super human powers) you may even find yourself struggling to master the habits outlined in these chapters. If so, not to worry—this is perfectly normal and definitely not a showstopper.

While the Personal Excellence part of the New Alpha program is designed to give you a strong foundation for long-term success, the reality is that even the most successful people struggle to make progress. Moreover, feeling negative emotions is (for better or worse . . .) totally normal when you're outside of your usual comfort zone. However, it's only by facing these feelings head on, and putting one foot in front of the other, that we actually make progress. This chapter, based on advice and ideas shared by New Alphas around the world, outlines the key psychological and organizational strategies that will help you to stay on track with the foundational habits that you've developed in Part I of this program and with the personal and team and organizational leadership competencies that you'll focus on in Parts II and III.

STAYING FOCUSED

Envision Achieving Your Goal

Take a moment or two to envision what it would be like to finally accomplish the goal that's in front of you. What would it look like? How would it feel? How would you or the world be different afterward? Why is it important for you to do this?

In the day-to-day drudgery of getting things done, it's easy to lose sight of our goals and priorities, but if you take a few minutes to pause and refocus on the larger picture, you'll allow yourself to tap back into your original motivations for taking this work on. Remembering why you're doing what you're doing will, in turn, increase your energy and enthusiasm for the task (or tasks) at hand, and it will help you prioritize the work ahead.

Write Down Your Top Goals

> *Yeah, I see that you have motivational sayings all over your office . . .*
> —MY DAD politely making fun of the fact that I post
> my goals, along with words of encouragement to myself,
> in places where I'll see them regularly

If you're having trouble making headway on a particular goal or task, try writing it down and posting it somewhere that you'll see it regularly (your bathroom mirror, your car, your computer desktop, the door to your house). I also often include words of encouragement and enthusiasm and a little artistic decoration to get myself pumped.

You might develop a mantra that you repeat every morning and every night, or even a song. Do what you need to do in order to stay focused and motivated, and don't worry about feeling silly for doing it. Learn to embrace your inner nerd.

OVERCOMING PROCRASTINATION

Commit to 15 Minutes a Day

If you're facing a big task and find yourself unable to stop procrastinating, try committing to sitting down for just 15 minutes and working on the task with the proviso that you're allowed to stop working on it if you have given a sincere effort for those 15 minutes. Entire doctoral dissertations have been written by following this strategy[1]—and it can be highly effective for people who (like me!) find that getting started is often the hardest part of a task.

In order to remember to actually do this, I usually put a note (in red ink or font!) on my daily planner next to tasks that I anticipate will be difficult to start. If I forget to leave the note, I'm much less likely to remember to use this strategy. (The procrastinating brain is very good at making us forget strategies that kill our procrastination urges . . .)

Identify One Thing That You Can Do Now

Similar to the 15-minute rule, identify *one* concrete action you can take now to move this project forward.

Forget all of the many things that it will take to achieve the larger goal. What is one thing that you can do in this moment to make progress in the right direction? Now do it and celebrate—and then think about what you can do next.

Make a Single Thing Nonnegotiable

Identify a single activity or task that you absolutely must complete in the next 24 hours: a *nonnegotiable*. Then, put this item ahead of sending that email that you need to send, or checking social media, or returning that phone call to Aunt Edna. If it's helpful, post a few encouraging sticky notes to remind you to do this one thing—your future self will appreciate your past self's encouraging words. Seriously.

You might also spend a minute in the morning when you wake up to just repeat to yourself, "I will . . ." and fill in the blank. Promise yourself that you will prioritize this objective, whatever it is, above all else. Don't answer the phone, don't go out for coffee with your friend, and don't go to bed until it's completed. If this involves an activity or action that you'd like to make a habit—keep using these tactics until you no longer need the regular reminders from your past self.[2]

Chunk out Your Work

If you find yourself feeling overwhelmed and stressed out by a big task or goal, try following this process:

1. Stop whatever you are doing.

2. Identify what your big goal is (for example, get a promotion).

3. Identify the tasks that need to be completed in order for you to achieve the big goal (for example, complete new payroll project).

4. Break down each of these tasks into smaller tasks and to-dos.

5. Pick the highest-leverage (the most important, timely, or relevant) item from this list, and do it now.

6. High five yourself, and set a date and time by which you'll pick another task or to-do to get moving on. If you find yourself struggling, you probably need to make your tasks and to-dos even smaller. As my friend and career coach Chand John, PhD, advises, "They should be so small and easy that you think to yourself, 'I can easily do this right now!'"

Explore Your Procrastination Habits

Are there certain times of the day or types of situations in which you tend to procrastinate more or less? What can you learn from these patterns of behavior that might help you to overcome your procrastination?

Sometimes, for me, procrastination is actually a sign that I'm worn out and need to quit working. Now that I've come to realize it as a sign that I'm out of energy, I try to give myself breaks when I need them instead of beating myself up for being lazy or unmotivated. I also try to schedule my less desirable activities during the times of the day when I know that I'm most likely to actually work on them productively—usually the mornings.

OPTIMIZING YOUR EFFICIENCY

Look for Multipliers

Jennifer Aaker, Stanford professor of marketing, suggests that *multipliers*—single activities that fulfill multiple goals—can be an effective solution for the time-strapped goal seeker.[3] For instance, if one of your goals involves spending more quality time with your partner and another one involves getting more exercise, then going on a weekend hike with your partner can fulfill both goals.

It's easy to resist the idea of multipliers, and they certainly don't work in every situation, but it's worth suspending disbelief and taking a few minutes to look through your list of tasks and routines to see if there's anything there that can be combined. For instance, I often listen to audio books while I'm out running—this helps me to meet my goal of running three times a week *and* my goal of reading at least one book a week.

Use Routines to Reduce Decision-Making Time and Increase Productivity

Routines are sequences of actions or steps that we follow regularly—often because they save us time. For instance, driving to a new job for the first time usually takes longer than it does after several weeks of making the commute. After a few weeks, you'll develop a routine around which route you take, such as when you change lanes for the exit that you need, which shortcuts to take, where to park, and so on.

When I write, I almost always wear blue jeans and a white t-shirt. The point is, routines can help us to achieve more with less time. Consider your daily activities. Are there any items that you can make into routines? Perhaps you can consolidate your email responses to one hour at the end of every day instead of answering them throughout the day, or maybe you can create an evening routine to help you end your day and get ready for bed more efficiently.

Keep a Time Diary

This strategy takes some work to implement, but it can be super illuminating and helpful. Starting tomorrow, set a timer to go off every hour. At the end of every hour, record on a sheet of paper what you did for the past hour. Review the sheet of paper at the end of the day. What types of activities are taking up your time—are they activities that further your long-term success, or are you simply responding to the needs of others *or* doing things on autopilot, without actually considering whether you should be doing them at all?

And don't forget that it's okay to say no to some requests. In the end, we're all just human beings and can only do so much with the time we have allotted. If it's helpful, keep in mind that recent research shows that people optimize their performance and minimize burnout when they remember to prioritize their own needs along with those of others. So, by saying no, you're actually producing better outcomes in the long run for everyone.[4] Similarly, it's not a bad idea to simply avoid people who are disrespectful of your time or who tend to drain your energy—this frees up time on your schedule *and* improves your emotional well-being.

Take Regular Breaks

Yes, it's important to work hard to achieve your goals, but it's also important to give yourself breaks to recharge during difficult tasks. In fact, research suggests that the *basic rest-activity cycle* is about 90 minutes for most people.[5] What this means is that even if we start off a task with gusto and energy, after about 90 minutes, we begin to feel tired and less focused. For this reason, it's not only okay but actually even *good* to take a break when you feel your energy flagging. Just be sure to set a limit on your break and fill this time with something that's not energy or soul sucking. (I recommend avoiding social media.)

For me, physical activity is really important, so I usually force myself to get up and walk around every 90 minutes or so. If I'm working from home, I'll take a break to play with my cats. Also, it's a good idea to build a few minutes of rest time into your day. For me, this usually means taking 10 to 15 minutes of rest time after 90 minutes of work, but some experts (who apparently don't work real jobs where taking 45-minute breaks is generally frowned upon) recommend even more than this. Your best bet is to schedule your lunch and break times around your rest-activity cycles. You could even work in trips to the office water cooler.

MANAGING YOUR MENTAL AND EMOTIONAL WELL-BEING

Celebrate the Small Wins!

Just as taking regular breaks can help to replenish and revive your energy levels, celebrating small wins as you progress toward your goal can be empowering and motivating. When you have a win, take a moment to congratulate yourself and maybe call your partner, parent, or best friend to share the good news!

I don't think buying yourself a ton of stuff as a reward is necessarily the right strategy here, but every now and again, it's okay to treat yourself to something nice (which may be free…) to celebrate.

If you're on a tight budget, even treating yourself to something as simple as a walk around your office, or a break to watch your favorite TV show, can be immensely rewarding. To some folks, this may sound like a lot of fluff, but more than just being a "feel good" activity, celebrating wins helps you stay focused and motivated while recognizing the progress that you're making toward what matters most to you.

Make a List of Things You Love

If you're going through a long period of working toward a big goal without much payoff, don't forget to take time to do the things you love. I used this strategy to survive my first (miserable) year of graduate school.

Take 5 to 10 minutes to jot down a list of things that you love and that bring you joy, post the list in a place where you can see it regularly, and when you're feeling down, pick an item at random from the list and do it. You'll be amazed at how uplifting and motivating this little trick can be.

Call on Your Circle of Support

Go back and look at the people whom you included in your *circle of support* (see Chapter 2, "Build Positive and Productive Relationships with

Others"), and consider the following: Whom can you call when you need a pep talk? Which person in your life is your greatest supporter? What is it that he or she does to make you feel reinvigorated and motivated? Call this person now!

For me, this person is usually my mom. My mom is such a cheerleader for me that she once sent me a pair of musical pompoms, and we had a phone conversation (across the country) where we each did a cheer with our pompoms from our respective homes. If anyone can pick me up and remind me of all of the reasons that I can achieve my goals, it's my mom. She really would have made an excellent therapist or life coach!

Consider WWMHD?

WWMHD = What Would My Hero Do?

Identify someone you admire (maybe you know her or maybe you just really like and respect her), and imagine what kind of encouragement or advice she would give you if you could speak with her about whatever you're currently feeling. If it helps, you can role play and pretend to be her giving advice to you.

Write Yourself a Letter of Encouragement

If you're struggling with a daunting goal or project or task, take 10 to 15 minutes to write yourself a letter of encouragement. Nothing fancy required, but be sure to list all of the reasons why you can achieve this goal. Be sure to mention the importance of continuous improvement—not striving to be perfect and avoid every mistake, but to always be learning, growing, and doing better.

If you wish, you can make it a postcard and mail it to yourself. I mail myself these types of letters from time to time and always love getting them back in the mail.

Get Creative and Play More

Play is the exultation of the possible.
—Martin Buber, Austrian-born Israeli Jewish philosopher

In the insanity of everyday life, it's easy to fall into a "work-only" mentality. While behaving like this can move us closer to our goals, it's also easy to overdo it and burn out.

In fact, even Einstein believed that "play" was an important part of the equation for success.[6] Current research also shows that the mere act of getting up and taking a walk can help us to be more creative.[7] As for me, I keep a stock of various art supplies around my house for times when I might need to take a break and nourish my creative side. Creativity doesn't have to entail fine art. You could try baking cookies, planting a flower garden, redecorating a room in your home—whatever appeals to you in the moment!

Remember, the Goal Is Progress, Not Perfection

Being high achieving can, paradoxically, prevent us from ever really going after our highest aspirations. This is because we get so used to "playing it safe" that we start to avoid anything that involves taking a risk, which of course means that we never achieve anything truly challenging or significant. (See "Embrace Failure and Continuous Improvement" in Chapter 4, "Develop a Mindset for Success.")

We also become terrified of failure, but for most of us, our failures are actually our greatest teachers. They give us ideas about what works and what doesn't. The goal is not to avoid failure but to fail fast and fail often[8]—and to pick ourselves up, and keep going until we accomplish what we've set out to accomplish.

Easier said then done, so I'll share a piece of advice that a good friend shared with me: "Wallow a bit, if you must, then put one foot in front of the other until you are out of the hole." In other words, allow yourself to feel badly, but not for too long—and then get your butt back out there in the arena. Also, don't be afraid to seek out others for advice and expertise—that's the New Alpha way!

Increase Your Happiness . . . by Doing Something for Someone Else

I'm not personally involved in AA (Alcoholics Anonymous), but I know a lot of people who are, and one of the things that I really appreciate about the AA philosophy is that service is a huge part of their program. Feeling sorry for yourself? Nothing cures that better than getting out there to do something for someone else. True story.

So, if you find yourself feeling melancholy or disenchanted with your vision or goals, stop moping, and make a list of concrete things that you can do to help someone else.

DEALING WITH CRITICISM

Haters gonna hate ...
—First articulated by 3LW, American pop music group; later evolved into a variety of hilarious memes that you can Google if you want a good laugh

It's unlikely that you'll get to this stage of the New Alpha program without experiencing at least some (if not a whole lot of) criticism from people you know. This criticism is likely to take on two dimensions: *supportive* or *unsupportive* in terms of the tone, and *helpful* or *unhelpful* in terms of the content (Table 5.1).

Obviously, you want to avoid the unsupportive and unhelpful people like the plague. These people are *haters* and will only make you feel bad about yourself and what you're doing. More often than not, they're also people who've tried to implement some sort of change or improvement in their life or leadership, failed initially, and then given up. The more similarities that exist between what you're doing and what they've tried (and failed) to do, the more vicious they'll be since any success that you have will remind them of their own failure. Interestingly, they may even be people whom you're friends with. These people might be good at a lot of things—making you laugh, managing the grill at a barbecue, or playing sloshball—but they are a destructive force when it comes to realizing your vision and goals, and I personally recommend taking care to avoid them when you're looking for feedback.

Then there are the people who love and support you no matter what but who aren't really going to have any useful advice for achieving your goals. These people are *affirmers,* and they're awesome to have around when you need a break from the stress and you want to feel good about yourself. Don't get me wrong, these people can play a really important role, but be mindful about relying on them too much for feedback since doing so is unlikely to actually push you toward your ultimate vision.

Table 5.1 **Forms of Criticism: Supportive, Unsupportive, Helpful, and Unhelpful**

	Unhelpful	Helpful
Unsupportive	**Haters:** These people are neither helpful nor supportive. They tend to be jealous and/or insecure, and they view any progress you make as a threat to them. These are often people who tried something once, failed, and gave up—and they resent seeing other people make progress where they didn't.	**Criticizers:** These people tend to be good at analyzing situations and finding fault, but they have trouble presenting it in a way that's ultimately constructive or motivating. They're useful to have around if you're feeling confident but you still want someone to poke holes in your vision and plans.
Supportive	**Affirmers:** These people aren't particularly helpful, but they support you as a person. They're good to have around when you need an emotional pep talk or boost, but they are less useful when it comes to getting honest and constructive feedback.	**Coaches:** These people are effective at analyzing a situation and recognizing both the weaknesses or threats *and* the strengths or opportunities. They also have the rare quality of being able to balance intellectual honesty and rigor with kindness and enthusiasm for your work. For this reason, they are generally very motivating people to be around.

Next, we have the *criticizers*. These are generally smart people who can easily see holes and logical flaws in plans, and they have no trouble sharing them with you. However, they aren't especially motivating *or* good at thinking about how to actually fix the problems that they spot. They tend to have high analytical abilities but lower *relationship management* skills. (See "Developing Emotional Intelligence" in Chapter 2, "Build Positive and Productive Relationships with Others.") However, if you can take the "heat" from them, they'll often provide useful feedback.

Finally, there are *coaches*. These fantastic creatures are a rare breed, but you'll know them when you find them because they'll give great advice about how to push your work forward *and* overcome obstacles. Coaches also tend to be highly motivating, and they are empowering people who inspire you to want to dig into the hard work ahead. Their approach is very much in line with the New Alpha philosophy, and their feedback is almost always the perfect blend of quality, honesty, empathy, and kindness. Coaches can be a powerful resource for getting high-quality feedback, but they can also be hard to find. And they tend to be very, very busy since so many people rely on them, so be gracious about their time if and when you reach out.

New Alpha Tip

You might notice some interesting overlap between the people that fit these four categories and the people in your *circle of support.* This is all normal, good, and useful to keep in mind as you move forward in this book and the program.

Congratulations on completing Part I, "Personal Excellence" of the New Alpha Program. You are now ready to begin Part II, "Personal Leadership."

PERSONAL LEADERSHIP

Building on the *personal excellence* competencies that you developed in the first part of this book, Part II, "Personal Leadership," will help you develop the knowledge, skills, and mindset to effectively lead *yourself*. You'll also gain experiences using the Vision-Plan-Execute (VPE) process, which will prepare you to lead and manage others in the third and final part of the New Alpha program: "Team and Organizational Leadership."

The chapters in this part of the program are organized as follows:

- Chapter 6, "Define Your *Personal Leadership Identity*," will help you to uncover the intrinsic aspects of your personality, and who you are that will help you cultivate personal fulfillment, achieve your goals, and maximize your impact.

- Chapter 7, "Identify Your Vision," focuses on the *Vision* phase of the VPE process, and is all about using the information from your *Personal Leadership Identity* (Chapter 6, "Define Your *Personal Leadership Identity*") to develop a vision for your ideal life.

- Chapter 8, "Develop Your Plan," centers on the *Plan* phase of the VPE process, and will enable you to craft a plan for your ideal and most impactful life—with particular emphasis on the year ahead.

- Chapter 9, "Execute Your Plan," outlines the third and final phase of the VPE process, which will help you to make your vision and plan a reality.

Taken as a whole, these chapters will help you to chart the course for your life, while also building essential competencies for turning ideas into action.

Sound good? Okay, let's go!

CHAPTER

6

Define Your *Personal Leadership Identity*

There is a vitality, a life force, an energy, a quickening that is translated through you into action, and because there is only one of you in all of time, this expression is unique. And if you block it, it will never exist through any other medium, and it will be lost.

—MARTHA GRAHAM,
American dancer and choreographer

Gael, a student from one of my workshops, recently came to me with a dilemma. He was just starting a new role at work, and, for the first time ever, he found himself managing a team of eight people. He was beyond excited for the growth opportunities that this new role offered, but he was also struggling to keep his team focused and productive. Since he'd assumed his new role, they seemed increasingly off task, and when he attempted to redirect them back to the work at hand, they either got frustrated with him, or they simply ignored him. He also admitted that he felt somewhat uncomfortable about managing people who just a few weeks before had been his peers, and he wasn't sure how to do this without everyone involved (himself included) feeling awkward.

"Hmmm . . . tell me a little bit more about what happens when you need someone to do something. How do you handle that?" I asked.

"Well, what happened the other day is fairly typical. One of my teammates was working on a report, when she was supposed to be making sales calls. I tried to address it indirectly by giving extra praise to those who were making sales calls, but she didn't even notice this, so I finally had to just ask her what she was doing and why, and then tell her, in no uncertain terms, that she needed to be making calls."

"What happened then?" I asked.

"Well, she seemed annoyed, but she finally stopped working on the report and got back to making calls—I mean she did get back to the high-priority task, but I feel like it caused unnecessary tension in our relationship and that she's just doing the work now because she feels like she has to, and not because she's engaged and wants to."

"Okay, let's zoom out for a moment. Think back to the activity that we did where you identified your *Personal Leadership Identity*. How would you describe your approach to leadership in three words?" I asked.

"That easy! I would say that I'm high energy, supportive, and funny," he answered.

"Okay," I responded. "Let's take a look at your new role. Do you feel like you're bringing those qualities to this role?"

"Wow—no, I guess I'm not. I think I'm so stressed about making sure that we hit our goals that I'm kind of erring on the side of being stern and commanding, when that's not actually who I am."

And therein lies the problem: Gael was focusing so hard on being the person that he thought he should be as a leader ("stern and commanding") that he was actually just coming across as inauthentic and awkward to his teammates. It's not that he was out of line for trying to correct his teammate's behavior when she was off task, because being able to do this effectively is a necessary leadership skill. It's that he did it in a way that didn't reflect his natural style.

In fact, everything he had done since assuming his new role was completely the opposite of his natural approach to leadership. Instead of being high energy and supportive, he was rigid and stern. Instead of using his natural sense of humor to get everyone laughing and enjoying the work, he was super serious all the time, and the result was that, rather than getting his team closer to their goals, they were losing steam.

Luckily, Gael recognized this and quickly changed his approach. At their next team meeting, he announced that their new team mascot was going to be the honey badger. Everyone laughed and quickly got on board. He reviewed the team goals and asked for feedback about how the honey badgers were going to tackle them. He also asked them for specific ideas about how he could best support them. And when he had to give constructive feedback to a team member, he made sure to frame it in terms of the group goals and his responsibility to support their work in the most effective way possible.

LEADING EFFECTIVELY WHILE BEING YOUR BEST AND MOST AUTHENTIC SELF

Put simply, Gael found a way to effectively lead and manage others *and* be his best and most authentic self—and this is the heart of being a New Alpha leader: discovering the intrinsic aspects of your personality and who you are that help you to experience joy in the work *and* success at the tasks and projects that you take on. In this chapter, you'll identify and explore the specific combination of talents and gifts that make up your own unique *Personal Leadership Identity*, including these:

- **Your personal values.** What you care about most in the world (examples: family, love, honesty)

- **Your character strengths.** Your best personal qualities or attributes—usually innate or related to your personality, rather than skills you've learned (examples: courage, persistence, kindness)

- **Your professional skills.** Abilities that you've gained by learning or training (examples: data analysis, writing poetry, surfing, teaching)

- **Your interests and passions.** Topics or subjects that interest, engage, or inspire you (examples: marine biology, saving the rainforests, soccer, Harry Potter, helping others)

- **Your ideal success conditions.** The circumstances or environment in which you do your best work and/or are the best version of yourself (examples: working alone in total silence, working as part of a team, working outdoors, working on a variety of tasks at once, working with a hard deadline)

Understanding your *Personal Leadership Identity* is important for two reasons. First, it will help you to recognize what types of activities, jobs, and life choices are going to help you *maximize your success*. The more alignment there is between your *Personal Leadership Identity* and what you do, the more likely it is that you'll be good at it and happy doing it. Even better though, enthusiasm is contagious, and when other people sense the genuine excitement and energy that you bring to the work, they'll be inspired and motivated to support and join you—which increases the ultimate *impact* of your work.

A FIVE-STEP PROCESS FOR FINDING AND INTERNALIZING YOUR *PERSONAL LEADERSHIP IDENTITY*

If you follow your bliss, you put yourself on a kind of track that has been there all the while, waiting for you, and the life that you ought to be living is the one you are living. Wherever you are—if you are following your bliss, you are enjoying that refreshment, that life within you, all the time.

—JOSEPH CAMPBELL,
American mythologist, writer, and lecturer

Step 1. List Your Accomplishments

Time estimate: Thirty to sixty minutes (can be spread out over several days)

Materials Needed

- A pen or pencil

To-Dos

- Under *My List of 20 Accomplishments*, in Figure 6.1, write down 20 of your life accomplishments. These can be activities or tasks that you completed successfully and that gave you a sense of pride and/or happiness. They can be from your professional life, volunteering, school, hobbies, family events, your childhood—whatever you want! The items on your list don't necessarily have to be things that other people would judge as "accomplishments." (Example: "I stood up to the class bully and got my butt kicked!" or "I passed my driver's test on the third try," though this last one might be specific to me....)

My List of 20 Accomplishments

Things at which *I succeeded* and that *gave me a sense of pride and/or happiness:*

1. schooling
2. family events leader
3. cooking
4. nutrition improve
5. kids - hs
6. craft rec +
7. partner w/ spouse
8. flex @ work
9. increased presence @ work
10. philanthropic involvement
11. leadership in NCL
12. learning arthritis
13. improve health
14. self improve - classes
15. 25 yrs marriage
16. join book club
17. with hold (?) judgment - kids
18.
19.
20.

Figure 6.1 My List of 20 Accomplishments

- I suggest you carry a notepad around for a few days while you're generating this list, email yourself from your phone if necessary, or write things down with bath crayons while you're in the tub. Do whatever you need to do to come up with your 20 items. And if you come up with more than 20, even better! Just make sure you get *at least 20 accomplishments written down* in the space provided in Figure 6.1, in no particular order.

- Try to be as *specific* and *concrete* as possible when you list each accomplishment. For example, writing down "Got 100 percent on a precalculus test in high school" is better than "Was good at math in school."

If you're feeling stuck (which is not uncommon with this activity), here are some examples from my list:

- I wrote two school plays that were performed while I was in elementary school.

- I was the second-fastest runner in my elementary school class.

- At the end of the year that I taught special education kindergarten, I had three students who could read more than 100 sight words each, when 30 sight words was the grade-level standard.

- One of my kindergarteners who started the year unable to speak a single word ended the year being able to say simple two-word sentences like "Bathroom, please."

- I won first place in the Big Sur River Run (a local 10K) when I was 10.

- I completed a half trail marathon.

- When I finished my PhD, my advisor, Professor David Brady, hooded me, and my whole family showed up to watch.

- My dad (who's very discerning!) loves my lemon meringue pies.

When you've completed step 1, move on to step 2.

Step 2. Analyze Your Accomplishments

Time estimate: Thirty to sixty minutes (can be spread out over several days)

Materials Needed

- Your completed list of accomplishments from step 1
- A pen or pencil

To-Dos

From your list of accomplishments, identify your top five accomplishments. (You can circle them, put a checkmark by them, or mark them some other way.) These may be your favorites from the list or the ones that are most important to you. Record your top five in the top row of the *My Top Five Accomplishments* in Figure 6.2. Then use the space provided to record your responses and/or notes to the following questions:

- **What does this accomplishment tell me about my *personal values*?** What do I care about and/or what matters most to me, based on this accomplishment? What am I unwilling to sacrifice, no matter what the situation? (If you're having trouble identifying the exact words for your values, Google "list of personal values," and see what words you find in the search results that might help you recognize your own values.)

- **What does this accomplishment tell me about my *character strengths*?** Which aspects of my personality or character really shine in this example? What does this accomplishment tell me about what I bring to the world, as a human being and as a member of my community and our global society?

- **What does this accomplishment tell me about my *professional skills*?** What can I do really well, based on this accomplishment? What special skills have I learned that helped me accomplish this? Do I have any special training (or something that I learned through school or a class) that helped me to accomplish this?

- **What does this accomplishment tell me about my *passions and interests*?** What kinds of topics or activities interest me the most, based on this accomplishment? What aspect of this accomplishment made me feel the most engaged or connected with my

MY TOP FIVE ACCOMPLISHMENTS

	Accomplishment 1: *schooling*
My values. What I care about most in the world (examples: family, love, and honesty).	Values: *education*
My character strengths. My best personal qualities or attributes. These are usually innate or related to personality, rather than skills that have been learned (examples: courage, persistence, and kindness).	Character strengths: *joy of learning*
My professional skills. Abilities that I've gained by learning or training (examples: data analysis, writing poetry, surfing, and teaching).	Professional skills: *research*
My interests and passions. Topics or subjects that interest, engage, or inspire me (examples: marine biology, saving the rainforests, soccer, Harry Potter, and helping others).	Interests and passions: *reading learning*
My ideal success conditions. The circumstances or environment in which I do my best work and/or in which I am the best version of myself (examples: working alone in total silence, working as part of a team, and working outdoors).	Ideal success conditions: *work alone*

Figure 6.2 My Top Five Accomplishments

Accomplishment 2: *listen to kids*	Accomplishment 3: *family events*	Accomplishment 4: *nutrition/cook*	Accomplishment 5: *work PT - balance*
Values: *family caring*	Values: *family*	Values: *health*	Values: *personal growth challenge*
Character strengths: *patience understanding*	Character strengths: *organization planning*	Character strengths: *learning flex*	Character strengths: *balance*
Professional skills: *analysis*	Professional skills: *cooking*	Professional skills: *creating with limitations*	Professional skills: *management*
Interests and passions: *together helpful*	Interests and passions: *together creating*	Interests and passions: *eating*	Interests and passions: *part of both worlds*
Ideal success conditions: *patience*	Ideal success conditions: *flexible*	Ideal success conditions: *in habit own kitchen*	Ideal success conditions: *small teams*

purpose in life? What do I love doing that helped me to achieve this? (If it's helpful, think of "passions" as similar in meaning to "interests"—but with greater intensity.)

- **What does this accomplishment tell me about my *ideal success conditions*?** What was the physical environment like during this experience (for example, quiet, loud, solitary, outdoors, in the car)? Was this a group accomplishment—if so, what was my role? Was this something that I'd spent some time preparing for, or was it more spontaneous? Was this a high-pressure situation or fairly relaxed? Was this a hands-on (applied) or idea-related (theoretical) accomplishment? Was I sitting, standing, moving, or doing some other physical activity when this accomplishment occurred? What time of day was it? (Consider any other details of the situation that you believe may have supported your success.)

New Alpha Tip

As you answer those questions, you might find that you're repeating the same words and ideas across the various categories—or even within the topics that were covered in Part I, "Personal Excellence." This is totally normal and will have zero negative implications for this activity, and it might even be helpful and illuminating!

On the other hand, it's also fine if you have no crossover between your categories. Just do what feels natural or right to you.

New Alpha Tip

If you're having a hard time answering any of these questions, or figuring out what to include for each category, take a look at the websites, books, and activities listed in *The New Alpha Resource Guide*.

Step 3. Hone in on Your *Personal Leadership Identity*

> *To be what we are, and to become what we are capable of becoming, is the only end in life.*
> —ROBERT LOUIS STEVENSON,
> Scottish novelist, poet, essayist, and travel writer

Time estimate: Thirty to sixty minutes

Materials Needed

- Your completed analysis of your top five accomplishments from step 2

- A pen or pencil

To-Dos

Take a look at the analysis that you completed in step 2. In this step, you'll synthesize this information in order to identify your (awesome and incomparable!) *Personal Leadership Identity*. This is the unique combination of qualities and traits that give *you* an edge and that help *you* stand out from the crowd.

Next, using the information from the analysis of your accomplishments that you completed in step 2, write down a list of your top 5 to 10 personal values, character strengths, professional skills, passions and interests, and ideal success conditions in the chart in Figure 6.3, "My *Personal Leadership Identity One-Pager.*" Do *not* fill in the *Personal Leadership Identity Statement* at the bottom just yet—we'll get to that in the next step.

One more thing, before we move onto step 4, take a look at your *Personal Leadership Identity One-Pager*, and consider the following questions:

- Is there anything that you feel should be included in these lists that's not? If so, add it.

- Is there anything on these lists that you think shouldn't be? If so, cross it off.

- Which aspects of your *Personal Leadership Identity* most closely resonate with what you learned in Part I, "Personal Excellence"? Put an asterisk (*) by those. (Note: These will likely be the aspects of Part I,

MY PERSONAL LEADERSHIP IDENTITY ONE-PAGER

My Personal Values	My Character Strengths	My Professional Skills	My Passions and Interests	My Ideal Success Conditions
1.	1.	1.	1.	1.
2.	2.	2.	2.	2.
3.	3.	3.	3.	3.
4.	4.	4.	4.	4.
5.	5.	5.	5.	5.
6.	6.	6.	6.	6.
7.	7.	7.	7.	7.
8.	8.	8.	8.	8.
9.	9.	9.	9.	9.
10.	10.	10.	10.	10.

My Personal Leadership Identity Statement:
Driven by [values], I use my [character strengths and professional skills] to [passions and interests].
Driven by [passions and interests], I use my [character strengths and professional skills] to [values].

Driven by health, I use my ability to cook & educate to help others with wellness journey

Figure 6.3 My *Personal Leadership Identity One-Pager*

Driver by   *use ability to listen to help attain goals*

"Personal Excellence" that you'll find it easy to adhere to. They may also be areas of strength for you on the self-assessments in Chapters 1 through 4.)

- Has anything else important come up in this activity or exercise? Make a note of it on your *Personal Leadership Identity One-Pager* as appropriate.

articulate a have goal

◊ post it on mirror
new / internalize

Step 4. Develop a *Personal Leadership Identity Statement*

Becoming a leader is synonymous with becoming yourself.
It is precisely that simple, and it is also that difficult.
—WARREN BENNIS, American scholar, organizational
consultant and author, widely regarded as a pioneer of the
contemporary field of leadership studies

Time estimate: Ten to thirty minutes

Materials Needed

- Your partially completed *Personal Leadership Identity One-Pager* from step 3

- A pen or pencil

To-Dos

Use the space at the bottom of your *Personal Leadership Identity One-Pager* to write out your *Personal Leadership Identity Statement*, which is basically a one-liner that quickly summarizes your distinctive edge as a leader (and, frankly, as a human being). I usually use one of the following structures:

- Driven by [values], I use my [character strengths and professional skills] to [passions and interests].

- Driven by [passions and interests], I use my [character strengths and professional skills] to [values].

Note that neither of those options includes a specific reference to ideal success conditions because I find that this part is usually implied, but you're welcome to add it in, if doing so is helpful to your process.

Also, if you want to check out a few examples, here are several *Personal Leadership Identity Statements* that students in my courses and workshops were kind enough to share:

Driven by the need to continually challenge myself and the desire to make an impact in people's lives, I use my resourcefulness, grit, and empathy to bring communities together through side-by-side learning and shared novel experiences.

—FAITH LIN, program manager at Cisco

Driven by my love of adventure and desire to help others, I use intellectual curiosity, patience, and teaching skills to teach outdoor wilderness survival skills to young adults.

—GERARDO, IT professional turned outdoor leadership instructor

Driven by a desire to create lasting improvements in people's lives, I use my persistence, intellectual curiosity, and statistics skills to research and teach others about poverty and inequality in the United States.

—HELENA, college professor

Congratulations! You've Successfully Uncovered Your Personal Leadership Identity! *(High Fives to You!)*

The information contained in your *Personal Leadership Identity Statement* and *One-Pager* describes a one-of-a-kind individual: *you*. I mean, think about it: how likely is it that even the most incredible, superstar person you can think of could have this exact same set of qualities and talents? I've run the calculations, and mathematically speaking, the chances are very slim. You are definitely the only you, and you owe it to the world to get out there and wield your *Personal Leadership Identity* as only you can!

If it's helpful, just remember this totally spot-on bit of advice that my mom once randomly shared with me: "You're never going to be the smartest, the funniest, the best, and the most popular person. Instead, you need to work on being the best version of yourself. Figure out what makes you genuinely different and special, and devote yourself to developing those assets. No one else will ever be as good as you at mastering that particular mix, and if you do it right, you'll be unstoppable." Pretty solid advice, Mom.

Concerned that you may have made a mistake, or might need to keep editing your *Personal Leadership Identity One-Pager*? No worries. Like everything else in the New Alpha framework, this is totally flexible, and you are encouraged to edit it as you grow and change and have new experiences. I've changed mine many times over the years—and I expect to continue changing and updating this as I grow and evolve as a person and as a leader.

Wondering if there's a place to list any potential weaknesses or areas of growth that you might bring to the table? Whoa there, overachiever. No worries—those aspects of your approach to leadership are addressed in other chapters. For now, bask in the radiant positivity of your *Personal Leadership Identity*.

Step 5. Internalize Your *Personal Leadership Identity Statement*

> *Everyone should carefully observe which way his heart draws him, and then choose that way with all his strength.*
> —Hasidic saying

Time estimate: Varies, but probably less than an hour

Materials Needed

- Your completed *Personal Leadership Identity One-Pager* from step 4

- Your imagination and ability to *think creatively* (See Chapter 4, "Develop a Mindset for Success.")

- Arts and crafts materials (for example, colored paper, markers, scissors, glue, pictures, stickers . . . really, anything that you have on hand)

To-Dos

Having your *Personal Leadership Identity Statement* down in print is important, but in order for it to be your foundation and your North Star in life, you also have to internalize it—make it a part of who you are. The key here is to spend time thinking about it and reviewing it regularly (multiple times a day for the first week or so, and at least once a day thereafter). In my experience, the best way to make this happen is to devote some time up front to exploring your *Personal Leadership Identity Statement* in a variety of (crafty!!) mediums. Here are some options for you to explore:

- Using some combination of markers, glitter pens, stickers, and whatever else you can think of, make a poster of your *Personal Leadership Identity Statement*. If you don't have poster paper handy, a plain piece of white paper will work.

- Cut out a postcard-sized piece of paper, then decorate it with your *Personal Leadership Identity Statement* (and whatever else is mailable), and mail it to yourself. (Yes, I have done this. I'm obsessed with getting mail, so for me this activity fulfills two loves: doing art and getting mail.)

- If you speak a second language, write out your *Personal Leadership Identity Statement* 10 times in your second language, and then post it where you can see it every day.

- Create a t-shirt, bumper sticker, or mug on Zazzle.com with your *Personal Leadership Identity Statement* on it. (I saw this on a bicyclist's shirt once, and it was awesome . . . so awesome that I rolled down my window and shouted, "I love your shirt!" He was thrilled and gave me a thumbs up.)

- Bake a cake or giant sheet cookie, and ice it with the text of your *Personal Leadership Identity Statement*.

- If you are like my brothers, all of whom are wholly obsessed with tattoos, get a tattoo of your *Personal Leadership Identity Statement*—or a symbol that represents it. Personally, I'd wait a few years until I really got it down pat before inking it into my epidermis, but I'm also squeamish about pain and permanent ink . . .

- Identify a song that resonates with your *Personal Leadership Identity Statement*, and then listen to it whenever you need a reminder of how great you are.

- Whatever else you can think up that's fun and safe. Email me your ideas!

DO NOW → → → → → → → → →

Pick two to three of the options listed above (or another option of your choice), and *do them* within the next 24 hours. Do as many additional internalizing activities as you need to until you can repeat your *Personal Leadership Identity Statement* in your sleep. At that point, it suffices to simply review it once a day. (I keep mine posted on my bathroom mirror where I see it when I brush my teeth in the morning.)

If at any point you find yourself "off track," or not living your best and most impactful life, go back to the list of options above and do two or three that will remind you who you are and what you bring to the world.

→ → → → → → → → → → → →

New Alpha Tip

For some reason, I've found it helpful to do the activities listed above that I most naturally want to avoid. Something about making myself uncomfortable in this activity makes me commit to it more readily. Take note of which of the options (or options not listed) seem most repulsive to you—and consider doing them.

Identify Your Vision

*If you don't know where you're going,
you might not get there.*
—Yogi Berra, American Major League
Baseball catcher, manager, and coach

"I just don't know what I'm doing wrong," my friend, Sofía, confided in me as we meandered our way along the beautiful Santa Cruz coastline one afternoon. "I've followed all the rules, got all the right credentials, and worked my butt off, and yet, I still feel totally off course and lost. It's as if nothing I'm doing with my life matters, or really makes a difference in the grand scheme of things."

"Well, what do you want to be doing with your life . . . I mean, long term?" I asked.

"I actually have no idea. I think I've just gotten so used to going into my office every day and working really hard, and getting promoted every few years, that I haven't really stopped to think about why I'm doing it—or how any of it even matters beyond simply getting a paycheck."

Sofía's story is a common one. You (maybe) graduate from college, get your first job, perhaps hop around a bit as you advance up the "success" ladder until one day you stop to look around and suddenly wonder whether any of what you're doing actually relates to what you want out of life or matters at all to anyone beyond yourself.

Trust me, if you haven't yet experienced this feeling, you will—and, not to worry, it's totally normal. In fact, this can be a great jumping off point for *identifying your vision*—an important competency for personal *and* group leadership that just happens to be the focus of this chapter and the first phase of the Vision-Plan-Execute process.

So what exactly do I mean when I say that you need to *identify your vision*? In essence, I mean that it's time to firm up your mental image of the future—understand where you're headed and decide how you're going to make your time here on earth count. If the idea of nailing down the next 60 to 80 years of your life seems a little overwhelming, daunting, or just plain impossible, don't worry! Your vision is allowed to be flexible, and the process for identifying it is actually pretty straightforward, and—if you're a personal improvement nerd like me—even fun!

In the sections that follow, we'll use the information from your *Personal Leadership Identity* (Chapter 6, "Define Your *Personal Leadership Identity*") to develop a vision for your ideal life. You will take into account how you want to live, what you want to experience or accomplish, and how you can act as a force for good in the world.

Also, since we're not ascetics or monks (well, most of us anyway), we'll cover other fun and even indulgent personal aspirations that you might have (like running a marathon, brewing beer in your tub, learning how to meditate, and more). In fact, making sure to incorporate these kinds of ideas and activities into your vision will *ensure* that you have enough joy and pleasure in your life to keep you energized and motivated through the challenges that you'll face as you work to realize your vision. Overachievers, fear not: you'll also have the opportunity in this process to identify any areas for growth or development that you want to focus on.

Learning how to identify your vision will not only help you to live your best, most fulfilling, and impactful life but it will also be essential to your experiences in leading other people. (See Chapter 10, "Identify the Vision.") The ability to identify an effective team or organizational vision will help you to influence and motivate a group of people toward a goal that's greater than what any one of you could accomplish alone. Piece of cake, right? Okay, let's dig in!

DEVELOPING A VISION FOR YOUR LIFE: HOW IT WORKS

Champions aren't made in the gyms. Champions are made from something they have deep inside them—a desire, a dream, a vision.
—MUHAMMAD ALI,
American professional boxer and activist

First things first: You're going to need a *vision board*, which is nothing more than a visual representation of your long-term dreams and aspirations. While it's true that simply putting together a visual representation of your dreams and aspirations isn't going to make them a reality (no matter what some guru tells you . . .), it's also the case that when you're creating anything, it's a good idea to flesh out the big picture (or vision) in advance. Instead of simply going through the motions of your day-to-day life without any real sense of direction, you need to know where you're headed. Having a well-thought-out vision for your life will help you clarify your goals, identify priorities, and make the right choices. Having a well-fleshed-out, visual representation of what matters most to you can also provide a little extra dose of inspiration on those days when you're feeling off track, defeated, or overwhelmed.

When combined with planning and implementation skills (which we'll cover in the following two chapters), visioning is one of the most powerful competencies of personal and group leadership—and one that even the smartest and most talented people often fall short on. So it's worth paying close attention to this chapter and opening yourself up to the power of dreaming big.

A FOUR-STEP PLAN FOR CRAFTING A VISION (AND VISION BOARD) FOR YOUR IDEAL LIFE

> *Never underestimate the power of dreams and the influence*
> *of the human spirit. We are all the same in this notion:*
> *the potential for greatness lives within each of us.*
> —WILMA RUDOLPH,
> American track and field sprinter

Step 1. Brainstorm Like Your Hair Is on Fire!

Time estimate: One hour

Materials Needed

- Your *Personal Leadership Identity Statement* and *One-Pager*

- A pen or pencil

- A highlighter (optional)

- The big-picture and dreamy part of your brain

To-Dos

- Do whatever it takes to put yourself in a relaxed, open, and authentic mood. Take a walk, enjoy a cup of tea, paint with acrylics, cuddle with your dog—whatever makes you feel calm, unblocked, and like your most relaxed and genuine self.

- Review your *Personal Leadership Identity Statement* and *One-Pager*. Use your highlighter to mark what particularly resonates with you right now.

- Pay close attention to any clues that you can glean from your *Personal Leadership Identity Statement* and *One-Pager* about how you might be able to contribute to the world in some way. Some examples of this are "I like making products that make people's lives easier" or "I enjoy being a part of organizations with a social mission." Jot down any thoughts that come to you here:

- Now, take a minute or two to think about how you want to live "your one wild and precious life."[1]

- For each topic below, start writing down what you'd like to do, see, experience, accomplish, achieve, change, improve, and affect in your most perfect, ideal, and mind-blowingly awesome life. Keep in mind that the most fulfilling (and ideal) life is one in which you build meaningful relationships with others and use your unique gifts to affect others for the better. Don't get caught up in the traditional Alpha ideology that success is equivalent to money and power—just focus on what would truly make you happy *and* give you a sense of meaning and purpose in your life.

- Write down, sketch, or doodle at least 10 ideas for each of the sections below. Feel free to include notes about what you'd like to improve, develop, or enhance in your life. Finally, don't think too hard about whether a particular idea is right or wrong—just list anything that comes to mind, and we'll worry about editing later. Remember, we are brainstorming!

Personal: Health and Wellness

Health and wellness are key parts of the New Alpha leadership philosophy. What health and wellness habits and practices do you see in your ideal life? Remember that it's okay to mention things that you currently do and want to maintain.

Consider things like exercise, eating well, getting sufficient sleep, drinking enough water, meditating, getting pregnant, limiting caffeine and alcohol, or even just taking a certain amount of "me time" each day.

Example. I want to exercise for at least 20 minutes a day every day.

Personal: Financial

Effectively managing your finances and paying off debt are important. How do your finances look in your ideal life? Consider any educational or other loans that you need to pay off and any charitable giving that you'd like to do. Don't forget to plan to stash away some money in savings and for retirement—as usual, your future self will thank you!

Remember that the focus here is on the money that you need to achieve your goals and lead a fulfilling and impactful life—not accumulating as much wealth as you can. Do your best to ignore the traditional Alpha myth that "money buys happiness." Remember, money is just a means to an end, and any book, program, or "teacher" that tells you otherwise is just trying to get you to buy what they're selling.

Example. I want to give at least $1,000 per year to social causes that I care about.

Personal: Fun and Recreation

Fun and recreation are key parts of effective stress management. What do you do for fun in your ideal life? Is it outdoors, indoors, by yourself, with others? Do you have any hobbies? What major adventures do you want to have in your life? Consider travel, experiences, and combinations of any and all of the above.

Example. I want to go on a yoga retreat with my mom in Bali.

Personal: Education and Development

In what areas of your life would you still like to learn and grow? Is there an interest or passion that you'd like to finally pursue? Would you like to go back to school, take a few continuing studies courses at your local university, attend a professional development workshop, or learn more about a topic that you're interested in?

Example. I want to take a course on how to use WordPress for my blog.

Personal: Spirituality and Transcendence

Whether you're religious or not, there's good evidence showing that feeling connected to something bigger than yourself can be a powerful part of the human experience.[2] What role does spirituality and/or transcendence play in your ideal life? What philosophical or religious beliefs and practices would you adopt in your ideal life in order to experience inner peace and harmony and/or connectedness with the world around you?

This may entail anything from church hopping to see if you can find a better spiritual fit, to volunteering to serve food to people who are less fortunate than you, to simply communing with nature more often.

Example. I want to spend 10 minutes each day meditating.

Relationships: Spouse or Life Partner

In some cases, our relationship with our spouse or life partner is the most important and meaningful relationship in our life. Is this a relationship that is or likely will be important to you in the future? Are you currently looking for this type of relationship or trying to improve upon (or continuously improve!) your current one? Either way, how would this type of relationship look in your ideal future?

Describe your ideal partner, your ideal relationship, and how you both act and feel in this relationship. It's a-okay if you're not looking for this type of relationship at the moment, or at all, but it's good to be honest with yourself up front about what you really want, so that you can prioritize accordingly.

Example. I want to have at least one three- to four-hour chunk of time each week with Nick to just have fun and not do work.

Relationships: Family

Family comes in many forms. In some cases, we're born into it; in others, we create it with the people we grow to know and love. How does your relationship with your family look in your ideal life?

Consider your parents, siblings, children, grandparents, in-laws, or even dear friends. How often do you communicate and visit with them? Is communication usually in person, on the phone, via email, or through social media? What are your relationships like—are you close, civil, best friends?

Example. I want my parents to know how much I love and appreciate them.

Relationships: Friends

What kind of people do you *choose* as friends in your ideal life? Are they like you, different from you, or a mix? Do they possess certain values, characteristics, skills, and interests? Are any of them the same folks from your *circle of support*? How do they make you feel when you're around them? How often do you see and talk with them? How do you stay in touch with them (for example, phone or Skype calls, dinner dates, weekend hikes, or notes in the mail)?

Example. At least once a week I want to spend time (on the phone or in person) with a good friend or someone I like and admire. (Rachel Brulé, this means you!)

Professional and Career Advancement

We spend a significant portion of our lives at work, so we might as well leverage this time to do as much good and build in as much joy as we can. Whether you're working now or hoping to find a gig in the future, what kind of professional life do you envision for yourself? What type of work are you doing? What is the work environment like? Is your work mostly solitary, or are you part of a team? Is the company well established or more of a startup—or do you work for yourself? Beyond your regular job, do you have a leadership role in your professional field? Be as specific as possible, but don't forget that you can always change this later.

Example. I want to be head of design at my current company.

Impact

British statesperson and U.K. Prime Minister Winston Churchill once fa-
mously said, "What is the use of living, if it be not to strive for noble causes
and to make this muddled world a better place for those who will live in it
after we are gone?" In an ideal world, how do you want to be remembered?
What is your desired impact? What do you want to give to the world and/
or your community? Do you give through your career and job, by volunteering your time, by giving money, by serving on a board, or by being involved in some sort of other group that creates a social or environmental
benefit? Are you invested in any particular causes (for example, animal
welfare or human rights)? What do you see as your civic responsibilities
(for example, voting, protesting, supporting political campaigns, writing
letters, or blogging), and how do you fulfill them?

Example. I want to start volunteering with the Sierra Club!

This is a huge to-do. If you got through all 10 of those topics, give yourself
a pat on the back, and take a short break.

Step 2. Refine Your Vision

Time estimate: One hour

Materials Needed

- The brainstorms (notes, sketches, and doodles) that you developed
  in step 1

- A highlighter or pen or pencil

To-Dos

- Go through each of the brainstorms that you created in step 1, and
  highlight, circle, or put a checkmark next to those ideas that you're
  pretty confident represent your ideal life. This may be every single
  item for each topic, or only a few. The basic idea here is that you
  should identify and make note of each and every idea that seems
  currently relevant to your ideal life. (It's also totally fine if there
  are things on your list that you realize, upon reflection, aren't really
  part of your ideal life. The whole point of brainstorming is to think

expansively, so kudos to you if you have items on your list that go a bit beyond what you really want for your ideal life.)

- Review your brainstorms. Do the items that you've highlighted or checked off align with Part I, "Personal Excellence," and your *Personal Leadership Identity Statement* and *One-Pager*? If so, great. If not, what do you need to add, edit, or delete? Take a good, hard look at the items that you highlighted from your brainstorms, and make sure that they conform with the New Alpha philosophy *and* who you are as an individual. In the end, you're the one who will have to put in the time and effort required to achieve this vision, so the content that drives your vision board should be authentic and motivating, while also challenging you to be the best version of yourself. (Your future self will thank you for being honest about this stuff now.)

- Transfer the highlighted or checked-off items from your brainstorms into Tables 7.1 and 7.2 on the following two pages.

Table 7.1 **My Ideas for My Ideal Life: Personal**

Personal: Health and Wellness	Personal: Financial	Personal: Fun and Recreation	Personal: Education and Development	Personal: Spirituality and Transcendence

Table 7.2 **My Ideas for My Ideal Life: Relationships, Professional and Career Advancement, and Impact**

Relationships: Romantic	Relationships: Family	Relationships: Friends	Professional and Career Advancement	Impact

Step 3. Turn Your Refined Vision into a Vision Board

There's no one single best method for taking all of the great ideas that you laid out in steps 1 and 2 and turning them into a vision board, so we'll cover a few options and variations, and you can experiment and pick the one that works best for you. Rest assured, your ultimate outcome here doesn't depend on which type of vision board you choose. So feel free to try one, and if it doesn't work, try another, or experiment with your own variations (and drop me a line if you hit on a good variation that's not listed here!).

Remember, there's no time limit, so it's okay to spend a few days or even a few weeks on this step. But keep Voltaire's famous advice in mind: don't let perfect be the enemy of the good. Also, I've found that many people (like me) tend to revisit this step many times (and for many years) after their first attempt, so don't feel like whatever you develop now is final and immutable.

Before you get started, you'll need to think of what vision board *format* is going to work best for you. Luckily, you have a few options.

Option 1. Picture or Collage Vision Board

How it works. You create a vision board from magazine clippings and pictures that represent your ideal life.

You should choose this option if . . . you have lots of pictures handy (for example, magazine clippings or photos) or access to a color printer with plenty of ink. It may take a bit more work than the other options, but if you're particularly artistic or visually oriented, then this is a great option.

Option 2. Mind Map Vision Board

How it works. You create a giant *mind map* vision board of your ideal life across various focal areas.

You should choose this option if . . . you don't have easy access to visual representations of your ideal life, if you're pressed for time, or if you prefer written words to pictures.

Option 3. Sticky-Note Vision Board

How it works. Using sticky notes, you create a vision board that represents your ideal life across various focal areas.

You should choose this option if . . . you don't have visual representations of your ideal life available, if you're just pressed for time, or if you love sticky notes (as my design-thinker friends do).

Option 4. Pinterest Vision Board

How it works. You create 10 Pinterest vision boards to represent your ideal life.

You should choose this option if . . . you prefer visual representations, but you don't have access to hands-on pictures that suit your needs. It's also helpful if you have some technical savvy (and by "technical savvy," I mean the ability to use a computer and search through a website).

Pick one of the four options listed above and skip ahead to that option in the text below. Also, feel free to try a few to see what works best for you.

Option 1. Create a Picture or Collage Vision Board
Time estimate: Two hours

Materials Needed

- The tables that you created in step 2

- Large poster board or butcher paper

- Markers

- Magazines or images of your ideal life and a color printer

- Sticky notes (optional)

- Scissors

- Glue or rubber cement

To-Dos

1. Get pictures, photos, or images from the Internet or magazines that represent the ideas from the tables that you created in step 2, and affix them by focal area on the poster board (see Figure 7.1).

2. Feel free to use a sticky-note placeholder for anything that you can't find a picture of (bonus points if you draw a picture of your idea on the sticky note).

3. If, upon further reflection, you decide that not every idea included in the previous tables is truly representative of your ideal life, then you can absolutely drop a few as you construct your vision board. Just be sure to include those ideas that resonate with Part I, "Personal Excellence," your *Personal Leadership Identity Statement* and *One-Pager*—and your gut.

Figure 7.1 Option 1: Picture or Collage Vision Board
Shared under a Creative Commons license by Kyle Pearce at bit.ly/2avcRGC.

4. Now stand back, admire your incredible artistic ability, and be sure to display your vision board somewhere that you'll see it every day—like on your closet door or the wall of your bedroom. The constant visual reminder will help keep you focused and motivated.

Option 2. Create a Mind Map Vision Board

Time estimate: One hour

Materials Needed

- The tables that you created in step 2
- Large poster board or butcher paper
- Markers (in a variety of colors, if possible)

To-Dos

1. Use your markers to draw 10 (approximately evenly distributed and spaced) circles on the poster board. Bonus points if you have enough markers to make each circle a different color.

2. Now, write one focal area from the list below in each circle:

  • Personal: Health and wellness

  • Personal: Financial

  • Personal: Fun and recreation

  • Personal: Education and development

  • Personal: Spirituality and transcendence

  • Relationships: Romantic

  • Relationships: Family

  • Relationships: Friends

  • Professional and career advancement

  • Impact

  Write each of the ideas from the tables that you created in step 2 around the appropriate circle on the poster board or butcher paper that you are using. For example, if one of the items is "get at least eight hours of sleep each night" and that belongs in the "personal: health and wellness" focal area, then write it down near the "personal: health and wellness" circle, and then draw a line connecting this idea to that circle.

  Figure 7.2 is an example from one of my early vision boards. (Note that my goal of eating five or more fruits and veggies a day was probably a bit low, but that's an area of growth for me, so it was ambitious!) Also, note that this vision board isn't perfect—I have messy handwriting, and I need to add more ideas—again, heed Voltaire's advice and don't let perfect be the enemy of the good.

  If, upon further reflection, you decide that not every idea that you included in the previous tables is truly representative of your ideal life, then you can absolutely drop a few as you construct your vision board—just be sure to include those ideas that resonate with Part I, "Personal Excellence," your *Personal Leadership Identity Statement*, and your *One-Pager*—and your gut.

3. Now stand back, admire your incredible verbal ability, and be sure to display your vision board somewhere that you'll see it every

Figure 7.2 Option 2: Mind Map Vision Board

day—like on your closet door or the wall of your bedroom. The constant visual reminder will help keep you focused and motivated.

Option 3. Create a Sticky-Note Vision Board

A little bit of wine and some Post-its can be a powerful combination.
—NICK, MY PARTNER AND FIANCÉ

Time estimate: One to two hours

Materials Needed

- The tables that you created in step 2

- Large poster board or butcher paper

- Sticky notes—ideally in 10 colors (not a deal breaker)

- A felt-tip marker (I like black felt-tip markers for this activity, but use what works for you.)

To-Dos

1. Using your felt-tip marker, label 10 (ideally different-colored) sticky notes as follows:

   - Personal: Health and wellness

   - Personal: Financial

   - Personal: Fun and recreation

   - Personal: Education and development

   - Personal: Spirituality and transcendence

   - Relationships: Romantic

   - Relationships: Family

   - Relationships: Friends

   - Professional and career advancement

   - Impact

2. Place these 10 sticky notes on your poster board. In a perfect world, they are all fairly evenly spread out across and around the board, but use your best judgment here.

3. Go through the tables that you created in step 2, and rewrite all of the relevant ideas from your lists onto the same color sticky note as its category header from the first to-do item in this list. Then place the sticky notes, by category, around their relevant category header on the poster board.

4. If, upon further reflection, you decide that not every idea included in the previous tables is truly representative of your ideal life, then you can absolutely drop a few as you construct your vision board. Just be sure to include those ideas that resonate with Part I, "Personal Excellence," your *Personal Leadership Identity Statement*, and your *One-Pager*—and your gut.

5. Now step back, enjoy the massive colorful clutter that is your dream, and be sure to display your vision board somewhere that you'll see it every day—like on your closet door or on the wall of

your bedroom. The constant visual reminder will help keep you focused and motivated.

Option 4. Create a Pinterest Vision Board
Time estimate: Two to three hours

Materials Needed

- The tables that you created in step 2

To-Dos

1. If you haven't already, sign up for a Pinterest account at www.pin terest.com.

2. Create 10 separate boards on Pinterest named for the 10 focal areas (Hint: Toggle to "yes" for "Keep it secret?" option if you don't want others to see what you're pinning.):

   - Personal: Health and wellness

   - Personal: Financial

   - Personal: Fun and recreation

   - Personal: Education and development

   - Personal: Spirituality and transcendence

   - Relationships: Romantic

   - Relationships: Family

   - Relationships: Friends

   - Professional and career advancement

   - Impact

   Now, go through the ideas on the tables that you created in step 2, and identify and select images on Pinterest to pin to each of the boards that you created in step 2 above.

3. If, upon further reflection, you decide that not every idea included in the previous tables is truly representative of your ideal life, then

you can absolutely drop a few as you construct your vision board. Just be sure to include those ideas that resonate with Part I, "Personal Excellence," your *Personal Leadership Identity Statement* and your *One-Pager*—and your gut.

4. When you're finished, take a look through all of your boards, and bask in the visual fulfillment. Since you don't have a hard copy of your personal vision, be sure to create a habit around reviewing your board on a regular basis (daily or several times per week). You can also print out your Pinterest vision boards on a high-quality color printer if you prefer. Whatever you do, having a constant visual reminder of your personal vision will help keep you focused and motivated.

Step 4. Maintenance

Be sure to regularly update your vision board; this will help keep you on track as you work toward your vision. You can make updates by adding pictures, written notes, sticky notes, or pins on your Pinterest board.

If it's helpful, keep a running list or folder of any new items that you want to add to your board, and put a reminder on your calendar or planner to update your board with items from the list or folder on a quarterly basis (or however often you prefer).

Okay—whew, you are finished with your vision (for now). In the next chapter (Chapter 8, "Develop Your Plan"), we'll work on making it a reality!

Develop Your Plan

A goal without a plan is just a wish.
—Antoine de Saint Exupéry,
French writer and aviator

A couple of years ago, two of my professional colleagues left their corporate tech jobs to pursue "passion projects," which in both cases involved consulting to business clients in their area of expertise. Both of
them are in their mid-thirties, and they have advanced degrees in fields
related to their expertise. One has been wildly successful and is building
a career around his passion, while the other is still struggling to get his
venture off the ground and to secure clients (and a steady income). The
main difference between these two people? The first knows how to plan,
and the second prefers to fly by the seat of his pants and hope for the best.
The obvious message of this cautionary tale: whether you love it or hate
it (and really either preference is fine), planning matters—big time. And
this chapter is all about helping you master this tricky, but important, leadership competency that makes up the second phase of the Vision-Plan-
Execute process.

More specifically, in the sections that follow, we'll build upon the vision that you fleshed out in the previous chapter and use it to craft a plan
for your ideal and most impactful life, with particular emphasis on the year
ahead.

DEVELOPING A PLAN: HOW IT WORKS

*Planning ahead is a measure of class. The rich and even
the middle class plan for future generations,
but the poor can plan ahead only a few weeks or days.*
—GLORIA STEINEM, American feminist and activist

As Ms. Steinem says in the quote above, planning is power, and if you can master it, then you can increase your power, and thus your influence, and thus your impact. With this in mind, the goal of this chapter is to spell out the process for making this happen, so that everyone, regardless of background or resources, has a blueprint for successful planning.

Sounds great, right?

Not so fast. For me and many of the people I work with, the process of *developing a plan*—or analyzing and breaking down the big ideas that we develop in the Vision phase, and translating them into priorities, goals, and tasks—is not something that comes naturally. If this describes you as well, don't worry. I've spent years talking with other New Alphas about how to simplify this process to ensure that *I'll* actually do it. And I promise you, it's not that bad.

With that said, if you find yourself struggling to get through it, I encourage you to just do the best that you can do and get it over with. Keep in mind that whenever I've tried to cheat and skip this step entirely, I've only succeeded in wasting loads more time, energy, and resources on the wrong things, such as focusing on the immediate and urgent, rather than the important, and often feeling both exhausted and defeated. In fact, there's an almost one-to-one correlation between the time and effort that I put into this phase of the process and the level of results I see:

More Time and Effort Now = Better Results Later

If on the other hand, you're a planning superstar and love this stuff— well, then get ready for a boatload of fun as this may very well be your favorite chapter thus far.

SIX STEPS TO TURN YOUR VISION INTO A WORKABLE PLAN OF ACTION

Tomorrow belongs only to the people who prepare for it today.
—MALCOLM X,
American Muslim minister and human rights activist

Materials Needed

- Your *Personal Leadership Identity Statement* (Chapter 6)

- Your *Personal Leadership Identity One-Pager* (Chapter 6)

- Your vision board (Chapter 7)

- Optional: The Tables 7.1 and 7.2 that you used to create your vision board (Chapter 7)

- *New Alpha Personal Planning Template*: a free download is available at http://www.LeadershipAndHumanPotential.com/Resources. FYI: We've made this a separate downloadable item because it's important to have something tangible that you can hang on your wall or bathroom mirror and refer to every day. You can print out and use this document for the next part, or if you don't want to download or print this document, there's a version of the template at the end of this chapter that you can use and then tear or cut out (see Figure 8.1).

Step 1. Set Your Anchors

- In the space provided on the *New Alpha Personal Planning Template*, write down the *Personal Leadership Identity Statement* that you developed in Chapter 6.

- Next, jot down any *guiding ideas* from Part I, "Personal Excellence," and/or your *Personal Leadership Identity One-Pager* that you want to focus on or use to your advantage in the upcoming year. This one is pretty flexible and is up to you. Personally, I list whatever I couldn't jam into my *Personal Leadership Identity Statement* and a few tidbits from Part I, "Personal Excellence," that I think will be useful for me to keep in mind as I work toward my vision. I wouldn't spend more than five minutes (at most!) on this part.

Here's what I listed as my guiding ideas: grit, balance, curiosity, empathy, initiative, innovation, continuous learning and failure, inclusiveness and team building, and integrity and moral courage.

Step 2. Identify Your Main Priorities

Next, based on your vision board and the items that you noted in step 1, identify your *top* two annual priorities for the year ahead. These should relate to the most important big ideas from your vision board that you want to focus on in the year ahead, and they can be phrased in general terms, such as "Improve my Spanish language skills." Some examples are "Find a new and more fulfilling job," "Spend more time with my family," and "Successfully launch the new product line at work." Keep in mind that your priorities can be fairly broad and general, and each one may encompass multiple goals, which we'll get to in a minute.

Also, as the examples above demonstrate, your top priorities can be personal, professional, or both. Resist the temptation to identify any more than two top priorities for the year ahead. As a wise New Alpha leader once told me, "You can focus on only two big things well; if you add a third, you'll bomb on all three of them." With that said, if you find that you fulfill one or both of these priorities before the year is over, then by all means, revisit this process, and identify new priorities.

For each priority, identify one or two big accomplishments that will move you closer to your vision. For example, if one of my priorities is "Spend more time with my family," two related accomplishments might be "Visit my parents at least every three months" and "Develop a system for not bringing work home from the office . . . ever." Sometimes, it can be hard to think about which accomplishments fulfill which priorities, so don't obsess over this. Instead, pick what comes naturally, and move on to the next step. You can always come back and tweak this part.

Step 3. Identify Your SMART Goals

Next, we'll turn the accomplishments that you identified in step 2 into SMART goals. What are SMART goals? I'm glad you asked! SMART goals are . . .

1. **Specific.** Your goal should state precisely what will be done. For example, let's say you want to run for president of the United States at some point in the future. Rather than saying, "Make progress on running for elected office," you might say, "Volunteer on at least one local political campaign in the next year."

2. **Measurable.** Measures allow you to track progress toward a goal. For our purposes, you should be able to look back on this goal in a year and say, "Yes, I definitely accomplished that" or "No, I definitely did not accomplish that." For example, instead of saying, "I'll learn more about political campaigns," you might say, "I'll take at least one course at my local community college on how political campaigns work" or "I will read at least three books that relate to political campaigns."

3. **Attainable.** It kind of goes without saying, but you need to actually be able to do whatever goal you set for yourself. A particular goal may be a stretch for you, but it should be *possible* for you to accomplish. For instance, unless you are already a pretty well known political figure, "Run for president" might not be an attainable goal for the upcoming year—not yet, anyway. However, "Volunteer for my local congressional representative" is probably attainable *and* is a step in the right direction in your master plan to conquer the White House.

4. **Relevant.** Be sure to pick goals that will ultimately get you closer to your long-term vision. For instance, "Run three times a week" is a fine annual goal, but it is not related to your long-term vision of "Being the president of the United States." So you need to either change it to be relevant to this vision or set a new priority for this year (perhaps something involving physical fitness or stress relief).

5. **Time bound.** Your goal should have an expected completion date—for our purposes, this should be within the next 12 months.

Write each of your SMART goals into the "My Annual Goals" grid on the *New Alpha Personal Planning Template*. (Ignore the "Tasks" for now—we'll get to those in step 4.) Here's an example to get you started with your SMART goals:

- **Annual priority (relates to some aspect of the long-term vision).** "Write a memoir."

- **Non-SMART annual goal.** "Journal on a regular basis." (attainable and relevant, but not specific, measurable, or time-bound)

- **SMART annual goal.** "By March 31, I will write in my journal three times per week for at least 20 minutes." (specific, measurable, attainable, relevant, time-bound)

Step 4. Make a List of Tasks for Each of Your Goals

Under the "Tasks" header for each of your annual goals, list the steps that you need to take, or the things that you need to do, in order to accomplish the goal. For example, if your annual goal is, "By December 31, I will complete at least one 10K race," then your tasks might include these: "buy running shoes, identify local running path, run up to one mile without stopping, run up to three miles without stopping, run up to six miles without stopping," and so on. If any single annual goal requires more than five to six tasks, then it may be better to break it down into multiple annual goals. Feel free to add specific timelines and deadlines to the tasks, if that's helpful for you. Either way, these tasks should be ones that you can complete within the next year.

New Alpha Tip

The more diligence you put into this step, the more likely you'll be to actually accomplish the annual goals that you've identified for yourself (even if you're just kind of guessing at the initial tasks). When I've left tasks blank or incomplete, I haven't usually achieved the goal.

There's also good research that supports the idea that planning for *how* you will actually accomplish something makes you more likely to accomplish it. With that said, your tasks don't have to be absolutely perfect. Just list what you think makes sense now, and remember that you can always go back later and edit your task list as you gain more clarity around the specific goal.

Step 5. Note Any Other Tasks or To-Dos for the Year Ahead

In the space below the annual goals grid, make note of any other tasks or to-dos that you'd like to accomplish (if possible) in the year ahead. These might be lower priority, but they are still important or fun or interesting aspirations that you'd like to work toward over the next 12 months, if time permits.

For example, my annual priorities might relate to work and family relationships, but I might include items like "Plant a garden" or "Go hang gliding" or "Visit Big Sur" under my tasks and to-dos for the year ahead. Including these items at the end of this document is a great way to keep track of the less critical projects and activities in your life that bring you joy or relaxation or that provide a nice break from the "heavy lifting" around the annual priorities and SMART goals.

Step 6. Review Your (Fabulous!) Work

- Take a look at all of your SMART goals and task lists. Does the information in this grid accurately reflect your *Personal Leadership Identity*, your annual priorities, and any aspects of Part I, "Personal Excellence," that you want to focus on in the upcoming year? If not, go back and edit what needs to be edited in order to create alignment here.

- Now, open up your *New Alpha Personal Excellence Tracker*. Does it capture all of the habits that you want to track and/or improve upon this year, including anything from your *New Alpha Personal Planning Template* document? Is there anything else that's missing? If so, add it. Is there anything that feels extraneous or unnecessary? If so, delete it.

- Make whatever other changes you need to in order to get your planning and tracking system in order. If you're not sure whether or not you need to change anything, not to worry—you can always come back to this later.

New Alpha Tip

Keep in mind that the planning process described in this chapter—much like an organization's *annual plan* (see Chapter 11, "Develop the Plan")—is designed to help you focus on the year ahead.

It's entirely possible, however, that you'll need more or less time to accomplish your specific priorities and goals. If that's the case, you should absolutely feel free to revisit your annual plan and make any adjustments or edits that are necessary. (You can do this as part of the *quarterly review process* that's described in Chapter 9, "Execute Your Plan.")

Congratulations, you are now one of the few people in this world who can effectively turn a vision into a plan. Woohoo!

MY NEW ALPHA PLAN

My *Personal Leadership Identity Statement*
Write your *Personal Leadership Identity Statement* (from Chapter 6) here:

Guiding Ideas from My *New Alpha Personal Excellence Tracker* and/or My *Personal Leadership Identity One-Pager*
Jot down any guiding ideas from your *New Alpha Personal Excellence Tracker* and/or your *Personal Leadership Identity One-Pager* that you want to focus on or leverage (use to your advantage) in the upcoming year:

My Annual Priorities and Projects
Based on your vision board, write down your top one or two priorities (including the relevant accomplishments) for the year ahead:

Priority 1:	
Accomplishment 1a:	Accomplishment 1b:

Priority 2:	
Accomplishment 2a:	Accomplishment 2b:

My Annual Goals

SMART Goal 1:	SMART Goal 2:
Tasks:	Tasks:
SMART Goal 3:	SMART Goal 4:
Tasks:	Tasks:

Other Tasks and To-Dos for the Year Ahead:

Figure 8.1 *New Alpha Personal Planning Template*

CHAPTER

9

Execute Your Plan

*We do not need magic to transform our world. We carry
all of the power we need inside ourselves already.*
—J.K. ROWLING, British novelist

Rob Strain is a 29-year-old superstar. After college, he joined Teach For
America, and within two years, he was promoted to a program director
position. Less than a year later, he was promoted again, this time to senior
managing director, and at age 28, he was promoted to a C-suite position
in the organization. As if all of that weren't enough, he also regularly does
volunteer work, and he makes time in his personal life for family, friends,
and travel. He's also just a totally fun and hilarious person to be around.

So what's Rob's secret sauce? How, by age 29, has he achieved a level
of success that some people never do?

Okay, confession time: In addition to being well aware of Rob's outstanding reputation through our shared network of friends and colleagues,
I also had the opportunity to supervise Rob early on in his career, so I can
tell you *exactly* what makes him stand out and why he keeps getting promoted. Simply put, Rob gets it done.

It doesn't matter how big or new or daunting the challenge (or how
short the time frame), Rob does a ridiculously good job of figuring out
what needs to be done and how to prioritize the critical work on his plate
so that he can keep moving forward. He's also mastered the psychological
aspects of achieving big goals, and he is capable of keeping himself (and
his team) motivated and energized through even significant challenges
and obstacles. In the entire time that I supervised him, I can't think of a

single instance in which he didn't achieve the goals that we set, and in true New Alpha style, he usually did so with *zest* and a *sense of humor*.

EXECUTING YOUR PLAN: HOW IT WORKS

One of the most common misconceptions that I hear from people struggling to achieve their goals is that high-achieving, fulfilled, and impactful people like Rob have some sort of "magical power" or innate ability that allows them to attain levels of success that simply aren't realistic for most people.

To be sure, *we live in a world that's objectively unfair.* I don't care what anyone says, it is 100 percent true that some people do have more advantages than others in terms of having greater resources, a stronger support system, or increased access to opportunities. All of these combined certainly gives them a leg up when it comes to achievement.[1] It's one of the deeply unjust truths about our society.

So, yes, we are all launching off from different starting points in our endeavors, and, let's be real, that makes a difference in terms of how hard we have to work and how far we have to go. But, in my experience, it's a mistake to think that, in addition to this, some people have a particular innate or divine aspect of their personality that allows them to be more successful than the rest of us. Frankly, that's just not true. To the degree that any of us are successful, it's because we're committed to *personal excellence*, we know who we are (*Personal Leadership Identity*), we can set a *vision*, we know how to *plan*—and we've *figured out how to get things done* (Vision-Plan-Execute). To that end, my goal in this chapter is to give you a formula that will help you bring your vision and plan to life and make the impact that only you can make in this world, regardless of your starting point.

Far from being a special gift that some of us just happen to possess, *executing* is all about having the right *processes* to realize your plan. New Alpha leaders take action in a timely manner and deprioritize or ignore those items that are less important. In this phase of the Vision-Plan-Execute process, you'll learn how to create a *personalized Daily Achievement Plan* and enhance the *review processes* that you're already using to monitor and improve your personal excellence habits in order to make sure that you're on track and making progress toward your vision and goals.

CREATING A *DAILY ACHIEVEMENT PLAN*

If you fail to plan, you are planning to fail!
—Benjamin Franklin,
U.S. statesperson and renowned polymath

Time estimate: Five to ten minutes per day

Materials Needed

- A piece of paper and a pen or a word processing document that you can access regularly (I use a Google Doc that I keep open at all times, but most people I know prefer pen and paper.)

First things first: Be sure that you're updating your *New Alpha Personal Excellence Tracker* every day. Personally, I spend 30 seconds doing this each morning when I wake up, but others may prefer to do it before bed each night. Either works, but figure out which option works better for you, and commit to doing it. Write a reminder on your calendar, write a sticky note to yourself—whatever you need to do to make this awesome ritual stick!

With that out of the way, here's the process for daily planning (which I recommend doing at the end of each day):

To-Dos

- Take out your paper and a pen, or open your word processing document. This is your *Daily Achievement Plan*.

- At the top of your *Daily Achievement Plan*, write tomorrow's date.

- Then write down "Daily Objectives," and list one to two tasks or to-dos that you would like to accomplish tomorrow. What actions can you take or what changes in your behavior can you make that will get you closer to your current goals and/or ultimate vision? What do you need to do in order to end the day feeling like you've been productive and accomplished something worthwhile? (Hint: These are most likely the items that you'll write in your *weekly check-ins*, which are explained in the next section.) Highlight these items in yellow.

- Now, look at your calendar for tomorrow. What appointments, meetings, plans, and urgent or important tasks are on your agenda for tomorrow? Write the times and events on your *Daily Achievement Plan*.

New Alpha Tip

Ideally, your *Daily Achievement Plan* is driven by daily objectives that *you* define for yourself. But sometimes, it's heavily shaped by external forces (like your boss or your kids), which is fine. Just make sure that you're doing everything in your power to make time to achieve *your* objectives as well.

For instance, in one previous role, I used to spend five to six hours of each workday in meetings (which were honestly not very useful or important). So I was constantly left with only a few hours per day to do the critical work that forwarded my vision and the organization's vision, on top of all the emails that I had to read and respond to. I felt really trapped and frustrated, and then one day it hit me: Did I really need to attend all of those meetings? Could I ask one of my teammates who was at the meeting to report back to me instead? Turns out that once I gave up my control-freak obsession with attending any and all relevant meetings, I had loads of time for other, higher-leverage, work. Did I miss a few important items that didn't get communicated to me after certain meetings? Probably. But did this affect my overall work? Nope. In fact, the quality of my work improved since I now had enough time to actually do it well.

Consider your daily objectives. Are these items that need to be scheduled in (for example, "Write a draft of the 'Execute Your Plan' chapter for *The New Alpha*"), or are they simply reminders to yourself about how you want to think or act (for example, "Remember to pause and think before you answer a question from your boss")? Schedule any items that need to be scheduled (including any notes, hints, and reminders to yourself).

When developing your *Daily Achievement Plan*, there are two key things to consider: (1) Try to schedule higher-priority items earlier in the day. This ensures that you'll actually get to them before all of your willpower, motivation, and energy are depleted. For example, I exercise almost every morning, but if I wait until later in the day, the chance that I'll skip this high-priority item increases dramatically.

(2) Think about periods in the day when your energy is at its peak. How can you capitalize on these pockets of time in order to do the type of work that requires this energy? Also, consider when in the day you have the least amount of energy. For instance, I have lower energy in the late afternoon. So if possible, I like to schedule meetings then—since seeing people is energizing to me and I'm unlikely to do very much productive independent work during that time anyway. On the other hand, I tend to have high energy early in the morning 7 to 9 a.m. or late in the evening (11 p.m. to 2 a.m.), so unless I'm okay with pulling a lot of late nights (which I'm not since I want to get my seven to nine hours of sleep!), if I have a high-priority item that's going to require intense focus and thought, I do it first thing in the morning. The same is true for any tasks or to-dos that I don't love doing. Of course, you have to find a way to make this mesh with your lifestyle and regular demands, so do what you need to do to make it work for you, and try not to worry too much if it's messy or imperfect.

- Write any key habits you identified in your *New Alpha Personal Excellence Tracker* into your *Daily Achievement Plan*. Start with the high-priority ones because lower-priority ones can go later in the day. For instance, I remind myself to stretch, prep my morning smoothie, and do my daily planning for the next day before bed each night.

- Do you have any extra space on your *Daily Achievement Plan*? If so, write in any additional to-dos. Just be sure to leave enough time for rest and relaxation. I generally schedule things only between 7 a.m. and 7 p.m. This time includes work projects but also exercise, meditation, getting ready for work, and so on.

FYI: I don't plan or schedule tasks or to-dos for Saturdays and Sundays (or any day that I take off from work). Other than my daily routines (journaling, exercising, meditating) and any outside activities (like my book club), I keep those days flexible and unscheduled. Am I less productive? Yes. Is that a good thing? Yes. Everyone needs some downtime, and you'll burn yourself out if you try to work like a maniac 24/7.

Example of My *Daily Achievement Plan*

7 to 7:30: Wake, eat, dress, complete *New Alpha Personal Excellence Tracker*, review daily and weekly objectives

7:30 to 8: Send any gratitudes, and write in journal

8 to 8:30: Meditate

8:30 to 9: Exercise

9 to 10: Shower, dress

10 to 12: Draft Chapter 9 of *The New Alpha*

12 to 2: Schedule blog post and newsletter

2 to 4: Work on client project

4 to 5: Update social media

5 to 6: Pick new health insurance

6 to 7: Work on to-dos below:

- Email client re deliverable dates

- Email Catherine H. thanks

- Pick bday gift for Dad

- Sign up for Chase Freedom rewards

- Email Radhika and Bitty

- Complete *Daily Achievement Plan* for tomorrow

7 to 9: Free time

9 to 10: Read, unwind

10: Sleep

New Alpha Tip

Rewriting or retyping a detailed *Daily Achievement Plan* every single day can be a huge time suck, so I keep a virtual "sticky note" on my computer's desktop with a *Master Daily Achievement Plan* that includes my usual schedule of activities, for each day of the week. (I also include all relevant tasks and routines.)

Then, I cut and paste this template into my *Daily Achievement Plan* for the day ahead and adjust it to make sure that it fits with whatever I need to do that day.

New Alpha Tip

What are some activities that you can do to keep yourself motivated and energized throughout your day? For me, these include things like calling my parents regularly (They're my biggest champions!), watching inspirational talks from experts in their fields, and exercising regularly. Make sure that you're building these kinds of activities into your *Daily Achievement Plan*.

A Note About Balancing Priorities and Going with the Flow

In truth, sometimes you won't stick to your *Daily Achievement Plan* exactly. Instead, your instincts will direct you to other tasks, and you'll end up running with them and not following your original plan. As long as doing so gets you closer to your goals, then that's fine. On the other hand, if you find yourself in the "flow" with the wrong (low-priority) activities, then you need to rethink your priorities and/or your approach.

Consider adding a column to your *New Alpha Personal Excellence Tracker* to track whether you're regularly achieving your daily goals. If you are, then kudos. If you're not, consider what you need to do (or not do) to get back on track.

Also, don't forget that no matter how great it is to be in the flow on your high-priority items, you will kick yourself later if you don't also take care of the necessities, like paying bills and meeting professional deadlines. It's all a very careful balancing act that you'll get better at over time.

REVIEWING PROGRESS

We cannot change what we are not aware of, and once we
are aware, we cannot help but change.
—SHERYL SANDBERG, American technology company
executive, activist, and author

Have you ever been involved with a group or organization that used a project plan? A *project plan* is basically the business equivalent of the ideal life plan that you designed in the previous chapter. And just as a business needs to review progress against the plan and adjust course as necessary, you're going to need a similar process for your personal plan.

I'll be honest, I spent a lot of time studying and interviewing New Alphas about this topic because it's not an aspect of execution that comes naturally to me. Luckily, it's actually pretty simple, and over time I developed a three-part check-in and review process that I use personally and with my clients:

- Part I: Weekly reviews

- Part II: Quarterly reviews

- Part III: Annual review and planning process

Part I. Weekly Reviews

Time estimate: Five to ten minutes (Once you get used to this process, it takes five minutes or less each week.)

Materials Needed

- A notebook and a pen

To-Dos

- Put a weekly reminder on your calendar to do your weekly review. Make it whatever day works best for you.

- Open your notebook, and write today's date and "Weekly Review" at the top.

- Write out and answer the following questions:

  - Did I achieve the previous week's objectives? *Typical answers: "Yes," "No," "Partially."*

  - Why or why not? *List all factors that supported or inhibited your progress toward weekly objectives.*

  - What went well this week? *List all successes and celebrations.*

  - What would you change or do differently if you could live through this week again? *List any errors that you would correct or changes that you'd make.*

- Now write out "Next Week's Objectives," and list all of your objectives for the upcoming week. These can either be specific tasks from your *New Alpha Personal Plan* that you want to accomplish in the next week ahead, or they can be smaller to-dos that, when taken together, will help you to accomplish the larger priorities and goals from this plan.

- Try your best to pick a reasonable number of objectives. If mine are all pretty small, then I might have five to six, but if they are large, then I might only have one or two. Use your best judgment here, and then adjust as you become more familiar with this process and learn more about what you can reasonably get done in a week.

New Alpha Tip

People ask me all the time whether their weekly objectives should be personal *or* related to their work, and the answer is that they can be either. If you're trying to be a rock star at your work, then by all means, list some professional objectives in your personal weekly check-in process. But if you're trying to focus more on the non-work-related aspects of your life, then the objectives in your weekly check-in process should focus more on those things.

(continued)

For me, these things ebb and flow as my circumstances change. If I'm in a really work intensive period, then my weekly objectives tend to be strictly professional. If I'm in a more relaxed period at work (where I can afford to coast a little), then I tend to focus on more personal objectives.

If it's helpful, in Figure 9.1 there is a picture of one of my weekly reviews. As you can see, it's quick and dirty and certainly nothing fancy—just enough to give me the info that I need to make improvements and identify my priorities for the week ahead.

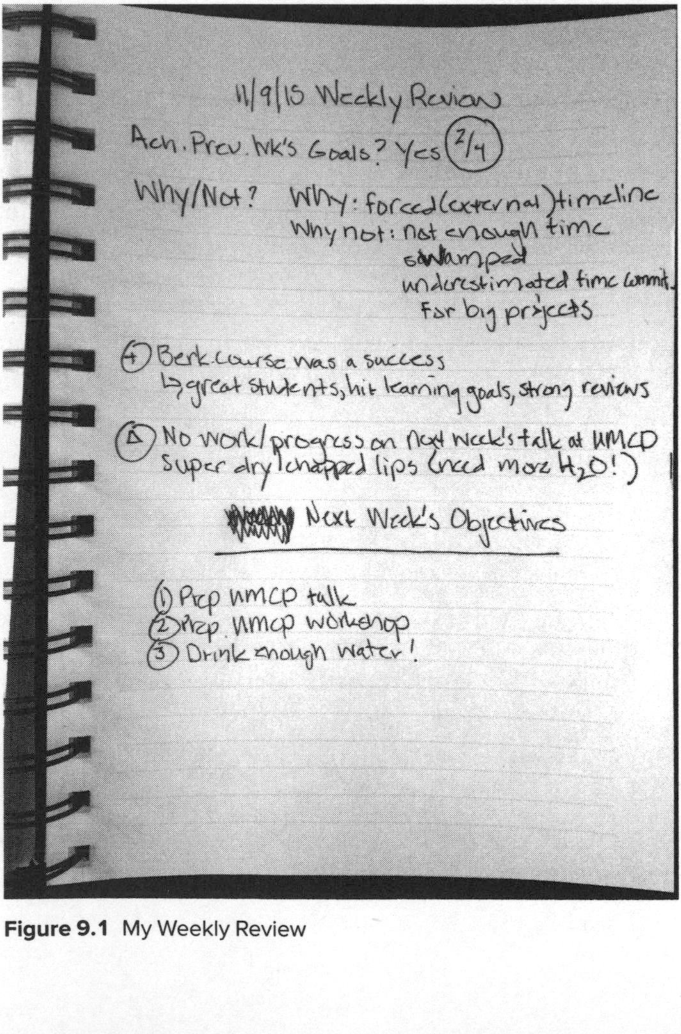

Figure 9.1 My Weekly Review

Part II. Quarterly Reviews

Time estimate: Five to ten minutes

Materials Needed

- A notebook and a pen (I use the same notebook that I use for the weekly check-ins.)

To-Dos

- Put a reminder on your calendar to do your *New Alpha Personal Plan* quarterly reviews. It doesn't matter when these occur as long as you do them about every three months.

- Open your notebook, and write today's date and "Quarterly Review" at the top.

- Write out and answer the following questions:

  - What went well over the past three months? *List all successes and celebrations, including any goals or priorities that have been met.*

  - What would you change or do differently if you could live through the last three months again? *List any changes or improvements that you'd like to make next time.*

- Now write out "Next Quarter's Goals," and list two to three goals or projects that you'd like to focus on in the upcoming quarter. These should come straight from the content that you included in your *New Alpha Personal Plan*. Or if you've already completed all of your goals and tasks (or fulfilled your annual priorities) from the plan, use this time to identify new ones. Remember that the goals you include in this part of your quarterly review should drive your daily and weekly objectives for the next quarter.

Part III. Annual Review and Planning

Time estimate: Three to four hours

Materials Needed

- A notebook and a pen

- Your vision board from the Vision phase (mostly for inspiration)

- Your completed *New Alpha Personal Plan*

Note: This may seem like a lot of time, but think of it this way: if you were organizing the annual plan for a high-functioning organization, you'd spend weeks or months on this. If you want to be a high-functioning individual and leader, it makes sense to devote some time and thought to this. Plus, you have to do it only once a year, and you can always chunk it out into small steps.

To-Dos

- Skim the weekly and quarterly reviews that you completed over the past year, and be sure that your *New Alpha Personal Excellence Tracker* is fully updated to reflect the current year's progress. Write out and answer the following questions:

  - What were your biggest successes, wins, or accomplishments over the past year? *Consider your* Personal Leadership Identity, *your priorities and goals, what you're most proud of, what brought you the most joy, and any big challenges that you tackled. The items that you list here might come from your celebrations board. (See "Embrace Failure and Continuous Improvement" in Chapter 4, "Develop a Mindset for Success.")*

  - What strengths or skills allowed you to accomplish your goals and wins this year? Did any aspects of your *Personal Leadership Identity* influence your successes? *Take a moment to update your* Personal Leadership Identity One-Pager *with any relevant new data that you can think of now.*

  - What were the biggest challenges that you faced this year?

  - What are the top three lessons that you learned this year?

  - What would you like to improve upon or further develop for next year?

  - What do you need to do in order to make these improvements? *Some examples for this might be personal development, coaching, additional education or training, or motivation.*

  - What goals, priorities, or aspects of your vision do you want to prioritize in the year ahead?

DEVELOP YOUR *NEW ALPHA PERSONAL PLAN* FOR NEXT YEAR

- Unless there are significant changes to your vision board (which is always possible), you can leave it alone for now, but feel free to keep it handy for inspiration, or update it with any new items that you think belong on it now.

- Download a fresh blank copy of the *New Alpha Personal Plan* template from www.LeadershipAndHumanPotential.com/Resources.

- Following the directions in Chapter 8, create a new plan for the year ahead.

And that, my friend, is how you execute like a champ! Now before I hear you complaining that this is a painstakingly detailed and time-consuming process, let me just say two things:

1. Once you get in the habit of daily planning and regular reviews, they are truly not that time-consuming (usually five minutes a day). They're just a pain to get started with because you're not familiar with them, and you're going to have to spend a few weeks figuring out how to make them work for you. They are, however, a wildly effective way to achieve whatever it is that you want to achieve, so I recommend at least giving them a try before deciding that they're not for you.

2. You don't have to replicate this process exactly as I've laid it out. For instance, your annual review and planning process might entail writing down 10 big things that you accomplished in the last year and 10 big things that you want to accomplish in the year ahead. Meanwhile your *Daily Achievement Plan* might be to write down one thing that you can do each day to work toward your vision and goals. If so, that's fine, and it's certainly better than not having any review process at all. The advice that I'm giving is based on what I've seen work for people who want to optimize the living daylights out of their time and work processes. But you can still find success

by adapting what I've described to meet your particular needs and preferences.

Congratulations on completing the Execute phase! At this point, you're now familiar with all of the basic competencies that are necessary to bring big ideas to life. In Part III, we'll focus on applying the Vision-Plan-Execute process to team and organizational leadership.

TEAM AND ORGANIZATIONAL LEADERSHIP

Building on what you learned in Part I, "Personal Excellence," and Part II, "Personal Leadership," in Part III you'll apply the Vision-Plan-Execute process in order to effectively lead and manage others:

- Chapter 10, "Identify the Vision," will help you to identify and communicate a compelling vision and build a culture that supports this vision.

- Chapter 11, "Develop the Plan," will walk you through the steps necessary to design a plan that will help your group bring the vision to life.

- Chapter 12, "Execute the Plan," will focus on what you can do to effectively influence and motivate others to turn the plan into reality.

- Chapter 13, "Sustaining Progress, Growth, and Motivation," will provide you with additional competencies that you'll need to keep your group on track and motivated throughout the Vision-Plan-Execute process.

This part of the New Alpha program is appropriate for anyone in a leadership role, but it will be particularly relevant to those who manage others (whether formally or informally). It will also be useful to those who wish to "manage up"—or "manage your manager"—in order to achieve your goals. Most experienced managers will be familiar with at least a few of the practices that are mentioned in this part of the book. But taking the time to work through the activities and exercises in these chapters will help you to strengthen your abilities, and it may even reinvigorate your energy and passion for the work, so it's time well spent.

Keep in mind that the Vision-Plan-Execute phases in this part of the program may not occur in exactly that order, and you may find that there's overlap and back-and-forth between the phases. This can happen when significant chunks of the work are outside of your control or when you are new to a role and some of the groundwork has already been laid. None of this is a problem per se, but it is helpful to monitor where you are in the process and to take actions that keep you moving forward.

While working through these chapters, also be aware that people tend to prefer certain phases of the Vision-Plan-Execute process more than others. (You may have already noticed your own preferences as you worked through the process in Part II, "Personal Leadership.") As a leader, preferring one aspect of the process more than others is fine, but it's useful to be aware of your preferences so that you don't inadvertently hang out in one phase for too long (and thus slow down your group's progress). Knowing your preferences here will also help you to select the team members and project partners who will best complement you.

Finally, a few quick notes on the language that's used in this part of the book:

- I use the word *group* to mean either a *team* or *organization* (whichever you're responsible for). I do this in sections where the content is relevant to anyone who leads others—whether it's a two-person team or an entire organization.

- I use the word *team* to mean the specific group of people that you manage, though I don't assume that you are the group's formal supervisor. For instance, maybe you are a team member who informally manages the group by virtue of your stellar leadership skills. If so, this content is still relevant to you.

- I use the word *manager* to mean any person who manages others, either in a formal capacity as their official *supervisor* or in an informal capacity, such as a *project manager* or *team lead*.

- At various points, I use the words *people*, *employees*, *team members*, and *your people* to mean the people whom you manage (either formally or informally).

- I use the word *work* to mean the activities that people do as part of their roles and responsibilities within the *group*.

- *Tasks* are specific pieces of the work that need to be completed. A group of *tasks* that are undertaken in service of a particular goal make up a *project*.

- *To-dos* are informal tasks that don't directly relate to any specific goals but still need to be completed.

10

Identify the Vision

*A vision is not just a picture of what could be; it is an appeal
to our better selves, a call to become something more.*
—ROSABETH MOSS KANTER, professor at
Harvard Business School and chair of the
Harvard University Advanced Leadership Initiative

Whenever people ask me about the best leaders I've ever personally worked with, Beth Napleton, executive director of the Chicago Collegiate Charter School, is always one of the first people who comes to mind. Beth and I both worked for Teach For America a few years back, and aside from her being highly competent and one of the most emotionally intelligent people I've ever met, when you work with Beth, you know where everyone is headed, you know how your work fits in, and you feel motivated and excited about the path ahead. In essence, Beth excels at identifying and communicating a *compelling vision*.

SIX STEPS FOR CRAFTING
A COMPELLING VISION

*The best and most beautiful things in the world cannot be
seen or even touched. They must be felt with the heart.*
—HELEN KELLER, American author,
political activist, and lecturer

The ability to craft a compelling vision is one of the foundations of effective and inspiring leadership. Interestingly, it's also one of the activities that people most often struggle with—and I can certainly understand why. When you think about it, "creating a vision" sounds pretty daunting—like something that only those in the realm of Cleopatra or Abraham Lincoln could really pull off well.

The reality, however, is that just about anyone can come up with a good vision, and the ability to do so is less about any innate "visionary" insight or ability, and more about knowing the right process. And in this section, we'll cover exactly what this process is in six easy-peasy steps.

Before we get started though, keep in mind that I'm going to describe this process as if you were starting with an entirely blank slate (with no previous vision in place), but you should absolutely adjust this process to best fit your particular situation.

Step 1. Identify the Scope of Your Vision

- Whom is the vision for? Is it for your entire organization or a team that you lead, or are you crafting a vision for your particular role in the organization? (This last one, by the way, is something that I recommend everyone do—whether you're the CEO or a summer intern.) Jot down your response in the space below:

- What is the time frame for this vision? Is it a vision for 50 years down the road, 10 years, 5 years, 1 year? There's no right answer here (and you might change your mind as you work through this process), but it's useful to have a rough timeline in mind to help frame your initial thinking. Jot down your response in the space below:

Step 2. Brainstorm the Future

This is a step that you, as the leader, can do in advance, or you can involve your team if you have one. There are plusses and minuses to both options. Personally, I find that involving other people in this step yields more creative ideas and builds early investment from key players, but it can also be more time-consuming and drawn out to do it this way, especially if you haven't taken the time to think much about it before involving others.

My recommendation is for you, as the leader, to come up with a handful of guiding ideas and then involve your team in this step in order to get some initial feedback and to fill in the details. Brainstorming might also entail simply having a series of conversations with other people (either on your team or within the organization) about their perspective on where the organization is headed.

If you are developing and launching an entirely new organization, it will be helpful to review your *personal vision* for any ideas that may also underlie the organizational vision. (See Chapter 7, "Identify Your Vision.") Ideally, regardless of where you work or what you do, the group vision should align with your personal vision and your *Personal Leadership Identity*. This doesn't necessarily happen immediately, but it's something that New Alphas are always proactively thinking about and working toward.

DO NOW → → → → → → → → →

Alone, or with others, answer these questions: Where is your group headed? How will the world be different or better when you realize this vision?

In the space below, list each and every idea that you come up with (no matter how off-the-wall):

→ → → → → → → → → → → →

Step 3. Pick the Best Ideas and Write a Draft of the Vision

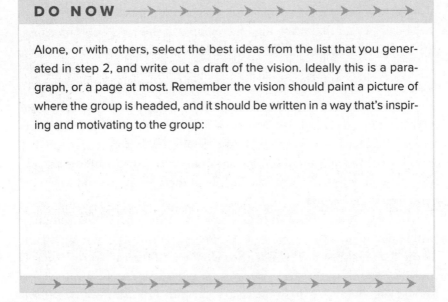

DO NOW

Alone, or with others, select the best ideas from the list that you generated in step 2, and write out a draft of the vision. Ideally this is a paragraph, or a page at most. Remember the vision should paint a picture of where the group is headed, and it should be written in a way that's inspiring and motivating to the group:

Step 4. Get Feedback and Make Updates

Circulate your draft vision to *stakeholders*. These are people who are invested in, or affected by, the work of the organization. Examples could be your supervisor, your team members, people you manage, customers, clients, investors, or board members.

Once you've collected and analyzed their feedback, make notes about what you want to change about the vision. What ideas are missing or need to be expanded upon?

New Alpha Tip

Try not to let this stage consume you or take up too much time. Listen to everyone's ideas, but also be aware that you're driving this and you don't have to incorporate every single piece of feedback that you get.

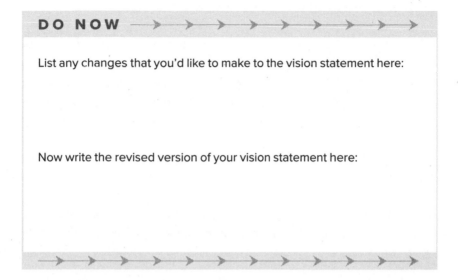

DO NOW

List any changes that you'd like to make to the vision statement here:

Now write the revised version of your vision statement here:

Step 5. Note Progress

Before you make the vision official, it's important to identify any past and current accomplishments that show progress toward this vision. This will help to build early momentum and get people excited.

So, for example, if you're the founder of a software company, and you already have your first prototype developed, first team member hired, or first investment secured, note these accomplishments.

DO NOW

Write down any past or current accomplishments that support your vision. Don't be overly modest. You don't have to make everything on this list public, but it's good to identify early wins since these initial successes will provide a strong mental and emotional foundation for the work ahead:

Step 6. Share (and Keep Sharing) the Vision

Once you've got the vision down on paper, it's time to get the word out to others. Depending on your role, you might be sharing the vision with the entire organization, with your team, your supervisor, or just close colleagues. Regardless of whether you manage or supervise others, having a vision for the portion of the work that you lead creates clarity and will help you to succeed in your role.

If you lead a group, here are a few additional tips that, *if done early and consistently*, will help you to build long-term buy-in around the vision:

1. Be enthusiastic and passionate about the vision. When people see that you're sincerely excited about where you're headed, they'll get excited too.

2. Get people to share (and reshare) what the vision means to them. At your next meeting or group event, ask people to take a moment to think about the vision and why it's important to them. If possible, share people's responses to this activity via email, a collage of sticky notes, posters, the company newsletter, or some other medium.

3. Share positive feedback from employees, customers, or others that shows progress toward the vision.

4. Be a walking advertisement for the vision. Bring it up on a regular basis, and always connect the group's work back to it. As a leader, your people look to you to see how serious or important this "vision stuff" really is. If they see that you take it seriously, they'll do the same.

DO NOW → → → → → → → → →

Make a list below of all of the ways that you can share (and keep sharing) the vision. When you're finished, calendar any tasks or to-dos, and communicate these ideas to anyone else who can be helpful in spreading the word. This last part is critical: enabling others to own and share the vision will ensure that it "spreads" more quickly, and will take some of the work off of your shoulders. It will also ensure that the vision exists and has meaning and impact even in your absence:

HELP YOUR PEOPLE CONNECT THEIR WORK TO THE VISION

If others can see it as I have seen it, then it may be called a vision rather than a dream.
—WILLIAM MORRIS, English textile designer, poet, novelist, translator, and socialist activist

Just as it's important to share (and keep sharing) the vision, individual team members need to clearly understand how their role fits into the larger vision. Having this information will give them a general sense of the direction of their work (which will make your life easier), and it will help them stay motivated and engaged.

With this in mind, as soon as you become a person's supervisor, manager, or team lead, make an appointment to meet with her to discuss her roles and responsibilities and how her work contributes to the vision. Rather than just telling her this information, give her time to share her ideas and views about the work that she does and how it supports the vision. Taking this approach now will help your people to better internalize the information in the long run.

You should also expect to have to repeat this conversation a few times before it really sticks. Team members (especially new ones) are often bombarded with boatloads of new information on a regular basis, and it's sometimes hard to know which information is more or less important.

DO NOW ⟶ ⟶ ⟶ ⟶ ⟶ ⟶ ⟶ ⟶ ⟶

List everyone on your team and how what they do contributes to the larger vision and plan for the organization. If you're the team leader, discuss these with your team members (to make sure everyone's aligned), and make a note to reiterate these connections on a regular basis:

⟶ ⟶ ⟶ ⟶ ⟶ ⟶ ⟶ ⟶ ⟶ ⟶

BUILD A CULTURE THAT SUPPORTS THE VISION

If you get the culture right, most of the other stuff like delivering great customer service or building a long-term enduring brand will just happen naturally on its own.
—Tony Hsieh, CEO of Zappos online shoe store

More than just making work "fun," successful cultures make people feel proud to be a part of the organization and encourage them to achieve organizational goals. This type of culture is a critical component of bringing the vision to life.

DO NOW ⟶ ⟶ ⟶ ⟶ ⟶ ⟶ ⟶ ⟶ ⟶

Make a list of organizations whose cultures you admire. What words come to mind when you think of these groups or companies? Jot down any and all ideas in the space below, and use these ideas to guide your thinking in the remaining learning activities for this section:

While each organizational culture is unique, based on my conversations with New Alphas across a variety of organizations, there are some actions that leaders at all levels can do to support a successful culture:

Hire Awesome People

Awesome people are the kind of employees who have the skills to do their jobs competently (or can learn them quickly), who are good colleagues (supportive, ethical, and so on), and who are easy to work with (on time, team players, and so on). As a leader, your role is to try to find people who are better at their jobs than you would be. This way, you won't have to spend too much time developing their skills, and they can immediately take ownership of their work.

Sometimes, for whatever reason (usually to do with funding limitations), you can't find an "A player" to do the work. In these cases, your job as a leader is to hire the best person you can find and then turn him into an A player through mentoring, coaching, training, and professional development.

Many of the most successful leaders I've encountered are those who are able to identify people who aren't quite at their full potential and who then develop them into superstars. It's easier said than done, but it can be a highly effective strategy for building a world-class team.

DO NOW

Given your organization's vision, what are your team's specific goals? Make a list here:

(continued)

What knowledge, skills, and mindsets do you need on your team in order to achieve these goals? Consider technical competencies and nontechnical competencies (like emotional intelligence, mindset, character and ethics, and ability to manage health and well-being). Write out your ideas here:

Given these competencies, write down the roles that constitute your dream team (for example, an engineer, a designer, or a finance person). List each role here:

Beyond writing and posting a job description for each of these roles, what actions can you take to find awesome people to fill these roles? (For example, ask current employees for referrals, attend meet-up groups for people who are specialists in these roles, or email contacts in your network to ask for referrals.)

Make the Work Meaningful

Besides contributing to an individual's sense of personal fulfillment, research shows that finding meaning in one's work increases motivation, engagement, job satisfaction, empowerment, organizational identification, career development, individual performance, and personal fulfillment. It's also been shown to decrease absenteeism and stress.[1]

This isn't to say that every single person should find meaning in every single aspect of her job, but our role as leaders is to help people to connect with their work in a way that gives them meaning and purpose on a personal level. When we're able to do this, our team members are intrinsically motivated to do great work—which makes leadership and management a lot easier.

DO NOW → → → → → → → → →

In Table 10.1, list the names of the people on your team. During your next one-on-one check-in with each person, make it a point to ask her about what aspects of her role or work she finds most meaningful or enjoyable. Also, ask her what you and/or she can do to make sure that she is finding meaning and purpose in her work. Record her answers in the grid below, and together, identify any next steps for her or for you.

By the way, some of the most interesting and powerful conversations that I have had with my team members have come from having this exact conversation. So even if you feel silly or uncomfortable initiating this conversation, I recommend giving it a shot and seeing how your team responds.

Table 10.1 **Conversations with Your Team or Staff Members About What's Meaningful in Their Work**

Name	Most Meaningful Aspects of Current Work	What We Can Do to Increase Meaning in Work	Next Steps
			(continued)

Name	Most Meaningful Aspects of Current Work	What We Can Do to Increase Meaning in Work	Next Steps

Empower Your People

Once people are clear on the vision and the part that they (and their team) play in bringing it to life, let them know what constitutes success, give them *ownership* of their goals, and then get out of their way!

Seriously.

Be clear about your expectations and then trust your people to get the work done in the best way that they see fit, and check progress regularly to ensure good communication and that everyone's on the same page. (See "Check Progress and Follow Up" in Chapter 12, "Execute the Plan," for more ideas on how you can do this.)

DO NOW

In the first column of Table 10.2, make a list of the people on your team.

In the second column, list their major roles and responsibilities, and circle any that you feel you (rather than they) currently have ownership of.

In the third column, list next steps for helping your individual team members to take ownership of any parts of their job that you currently own. This may be as simple as having a frank conversation with them, or it may involve a more formal plan to gradually release responsibility to them.

Table 10.2 **Progress on Empowering Your Team or Staff Members**

Name	Major Roles and Responsibilities	Next Steps for Transferring Ownership

Establish, Model, and Enforce Group Norms

Establish group norms. On your own, or with members of your team, answer the following question: when we're at our best, how do we act and interact with one another? There's no one best set of norms, but it's useful to consider any core values (see the discussion of *values* in Chapter 6, "Define Your *Personal Leadership Identity*") and ethical principles (Chapter 1, "Demonstrate Character and Ethics") that you'd like to guide the decisions and behaviors of your group. You can also ask your team for suggestions here. Keep in mind that these norms will often change and evolve over time as you gain more experience working together.

DO NOW → → → → → → → → → →

Use the space below to list a few norms that you might like to adopt. (I've listed two of my favorites to get you started):

- We operate with generosity of spirit. (We assume the best and ask probing questions when we're confused about someone's actions or words.)

- We support one another as people and professionals.

→ → → → → → → → → → → →

Model group norms. It's not enough to just set norms. You have to show that you're serious about them. Make sure you are acting in accordance with your team and organization's norms at all times. Verbalize them as much as possible, even if doing so makes you feel awkward.

For instance, if one of your norms is to support one another as people and professionals, and someone on your team comes to you because he is feeling overwhelmed and needs help setting priorities, you might say something like, "I want to support you as a person and professional. Let's come up with a list of ideas for how I might do this."

It may feel silly in the beginning, but people *love* it. By doing this consistently and earnestly, within a few weeks you'll see other people on your team starting to throw around the language of the norms in regular conversations—which is a magical and deeply satisfying experience for any leader.

DO NOW →→→→→→→→→→

List each of your team norms below. Beside each one, identify two to three ways that you can embody this norm at work. Make a note on your calendar or planner to implement one idea each day for the next three weeks, or until you feel that you've fully absorbed each of the norms into your everyday behaviors and actions:

Enforce group norms. If you see someone acting in a way that doesn't support your group norms, then make it a point to talk with her about it—ideally, in private, so as not to embarrass her.

Another great idea is to call yourself out when you inadvertently violate a norm or aspect of the group culture. Don't overapologize for this violation, but make a point to recognize the error and express your desire to do better. This will serve the dual purpose of making you relatable to your team (so you don't come across as out of touch or preachy) and underscoring the group norms. It also makes it easier to call people out on this if they've seen that you're willing to call out yourself too.

Celebrate Wins

It's a little-known fact that everyone (even the most wildly successful and seemingly confident person) needs a pat on the back every now and again. Celebrating wins, or milestones that mark significant progress toward goals, is a great way to do this.

Besides making people feel good about the work, which can be highly motivating, celebrating wins also gives people feedback about what they should keep doing. Moreover, it helps them reflect on what's been accomplished so far and prepares them for what's coming next. Finally, it builds team camaraderie and the feeling that "we're all in this together, and we can do it!"

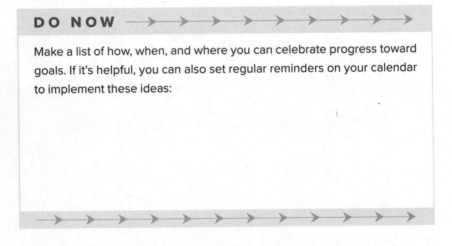

DO NOW

Make a list of how, when, and where you can celebrate progress toward goals. If it's helpful, you can also set regular reminders on your calendar to implement these ideas:

Let People Know That You Value and Care About Them

If you want people to feel motivated to do their best work, be clear about why you value their contributions to the team *and* make sure that they know that you care about them as individuals (beyond whatever professional competencies they bring to the table).

You're probably not going to be everybody's best friend (professional boundaries can be a good thing!), and you're going to piss off a few people from time to time. But your employees should know that they are more than just cogs in a wheel and that you value and appreciate them in a holistic sense.

DO NOW

How have supervisors made you feel valued and/or cared about in the past? Make a list here:

What actions can you take to let your team know that you value their work contributions and care about them as people? List your ideas here:

Model Transparency and Continuous Improvement

Most people have some natural resistance to change, and this is especially true when they've experienced a slew of unproductive and time-sucking changes in the past.

With this in mind, as a leader, when you make any kind of change or implement a new system, policy, or procedure, be sure to give people a rationale for *why* the change is occurring *and* the problem that it's designed to alleviate. (Ideally, this is a problem that, if resolved, will make their lives easier.) It's incredible how much more open to change people are when they understand the reasoning behind it and they feel like their needs and wants are being considered.

Also, be open to feedback about the change. You can't please everyone, but if you listen to people, and communicate that you hear what they're saying and are trying to create improvements, people will usually at least respect your efforts.

DO NOW → → → → → → → → →

In the first column of Table 10.3, make a list of any changes or new initiatives that you've introduced in the past year.

In the second column, list what went well in terms of implementation.

In the third column, list what you could have done before, during, or after the change to make it more enticing to the people affected. Keep the ideas from the third column in mind when you design and implement future changes.

Table 10.3 **Conversations with Your Team or Staff Members on Changes and New Initiatives**

Name or Description of New Initiative	What Went Well	What Could Be Changed or Improved

Name or Description of New Initiative	What Went Well	What Could Be Changed or Improved

STAY CURRENT

Knowledge is power.
—Variously attributed

Whether you're running an organization or you're in your first job out of school (or maybe doing both!), staying on top of any information that relates to your work, your organization, and the broader field or industry will give you the background information that you need to do your job well—and to lead your team to success.

For example, I remember sitting in a work meeting once where we were trying to figure out how to contact someone whom we wanted to invite to speak at one of our events. The problem was that this person had recently left her position at a large well-known organization, and no one knew how to contact her now that she was no longer with the organization. Suddenly one of our interns shouted out the answer: the person we wanted to contact had moved to a competing organization and would be starting her new role in a month.

How did the intern know this? Anticipating that we might want to have her speak at this event (see "Be Proactive" in Chapter 4, "Develop a Mindset for Success"), he had followed her on Twitter a few weeks before and he had been reading her updates regularly. It was an impressive moment, and it definitely got the attention of everyone in the room.

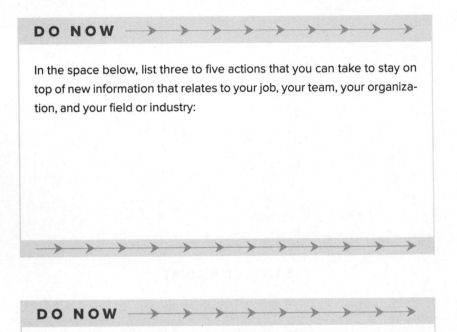

DO NOW

In the space below, list three to five actions that you can take to stay on top of new information that relates to your job, your team, your organization, and your field or industry:

DO NOW

Set a Google Alert (https://www.google.com/alerts) to notify you every time a particular word or topic that relates to your job, organization, or professional field comes up in new search results.

CHAPTER

11

Develop the Plan

Our goals can only be reached through a vehicle of a plan, in which we must fervently believe, and upon which we must vigorously act. There is no other route to success.
—Pablo Picasso, Spanish painter, sculptor, printmaker, ceramicist, stage designer, poet, and playwright

"So what's the plan for organizing the teacher testing in Atlanta?" my boss, Alison Banks (then managing director of admissions for Teach For America), asked me. The year was 2006, and I was working with Teach For America's admissions team to organize the teacher certification testing process for new corps members across the United States.

"Um, I'm going to ask Dena to coordinate the testing in Atlanta, since I'll be working in Houston at that point," I responded (while silently congratulating myself for figuring out how to pull off two simultaneous testing sessions nearly 800 miles apart).

"Okay, that's a good idea, but that's not a plan. A plan includes detailed information about what needs to get done, including specific tasks and timelines. Dena has no background in this, so you need to spell out exactly what she needs to do by when in order to meet the goals for this project. Do you understand?" Alison asked me. I did—and I immediately returned to my desk where I wrote up a detailed plan for Dena so that she knew what needed to be done by when in order to make the Atlanta trip a success.

I'm embarrassed to admit this, but until that conversation, I had never actually recognized the difference between having an *idea* about how something should work and developing a concrete *plan* for how it should actually play out. It sounds so basic, but that simple conversation changed my life. Since that time, I've worked with and studied leaders across a variety of fields and industries who have mastered this competency (probably far sooner than I did), and this chapter is specifically designed to help *you* develop the competencies necessary to rock this phase of the Vision-Plan-Execute process.

Here are two pieces of advice before we get started. First, if you're like me and don't love this part of the Vision-Plan-Execute process, it can be tempting to simply write it off by saying something like, "Well, we can't have a plan yet because we don't have enough information, and it will change anyway, so why bother?"

Unfortunately, a fair number of leaders do exactly this, but I can tell you from experience (and from coaching their exasperated colleagues and team members) that not having a plan is a mistake. The process of developing a plan forces you to think through the details of *how* you'll actually realize your vision, and if you skip this part of the process, you'll likely just waste time spinning your wheels, which is a great way to frustrate yourself and everyone around you.

Plus, even if the plan does evolve and need changing, it's *much* easier and more efficient to change an already existing plan (and see how all of the rest of the work is affected by each pivot or tweak) than to continuously dump more work onto an already vague and amorphous bunch of projects and tasks with unclear interdependencies.

Much like the Plan phase in Part II, "Personal Leadership," putting some time and energy into this phase will pay off for you and your team in the long run. And don't worry if you struggle with this at the outset. That's normal. I've gone through this process numerous times, both as a leader and as a consultant and coach, and I still occasionally struggle with it . The good news is that it definitely gets easier over time. Also, once you've gone through it once or twice, you'll start to develop ideas about what works better or worse, and you can adapt the process in the way that works best for you and your team.

SIX STEPS TO TURN YOUR VISION INTO A WORKABLE PLAN OF ACTION

*Planning is bringing the future into the present
so that you can do something about it now.*
—ALAN LAKEIN, American author and
expert on time management

Developing a workable team or organizational plan involves the same steps that you used to develop a personal plan in Part II, "Personal Leadership." The only difference is that, depending on your role in the group, you may want to involve others in this process (whereas you wouldn't necessarily do that in creating and maintaining your *New Alpha Personal Plan*).

Also, keep in mind that the process described in this chapter is designed to help you create a plan for the year ahead, but you can easily adjust the timeline to fit your specific needs and situation.

Step 1. Set Your Anchors

First things first: make note of any key aspects of the vision that you developed in Chapter 10 that will "anchor" the plan. This should include elements of the group's culture or norms that will support the work ahead. It should also outline a general idea of the *strategy* that you will pursue over the long term in order to realize the ultimate vision.

For instance, if your group's vision is to ensure that every person in the world has access to clean drinking water, your strategy might be to form groups of people who build wells in areas where access to clean water is limited, or it might involve distributing filters that people can use to clean water. The point is that you need to hone in on the long-term angle or approach that you'll take to achieve your vision, and you need to nail it down now.

Lastly, if your goal for this chapter is to develop an individualized plan for the portion of the organizational or team vision that you're personally responsible for, make note of any aspects of Part I, "Personal Excellence," or your *Personal Leadership Identity* that will anchor your work for the next 12 months.

DO NOW →→→→→→→→→→→

What aspects of your group's culture or norms will support the work ahead?

What is your strategy for achieving the vision? Put another way, of all the possible routes to achieving the vision, which one will your group pursue?

Optional: Which aspects of Part I, "Personal Excellence," or your *Personal Leadership Identity* will anchor your work for the next 12 months?

Step 2. Identify the Main Priorities

Once your anchors are in place, you'll want to identify the main priorities for the year ahead. Priorities shouldn't encompass every last detail of the work—just the high-level activities that align with the strategy and that, if prioritized, will help you and your team to make progress toward the vision.

DO NOW →→→→→→→→→

List your main priorities for the year ahead in the *New Alpha Team and Organizational Planning Template*, which is included at the end of this chapter (Figure 11.1) and which can be downloaded from www.Leadership

AndHumanPotential.com/Resources. If you have more than three priorities, you can print out multiple copies of this document or edit the document itself.

Step 3. Identify SMART Goals

List the SMART (specific, measurable, attainable, relevant, time-bound) goals that need to be achieved over the next year in order to accomplish each priority (see "Step 3, Identify Your SMART Goals," in Chapter 8, "Develop Your Plan"). In the clean water example, a SMART annual goal might be "We will research, vet, and establish contracts with three site partners in Ethiopia in the next 12 months." As you work to flesh out your goal, keep in mind that it's not uncommon to have multiple goals for a single priority.

DO NOW

For each priority that you listed on the *New Alpha Team and Organizational Planning Template*, write out the relevant SMART goals in the middle column.

Step 4. Make a List of Tasks for Each Goal

Here's where we get into the nitty-gritty. For each annual goal that you identified in step 3, make a list of the tasks that need to be completed in order to accomplish the goal. Keep in mind that sometimes the "tasks" that you identify are actually "projects" that need to be broken down into component tasks.

People often want to know how "granular" they should be with their tasks, and the answer is that there is no one best way to do this. Some groups work better with extremely well specified tasks, and some prefer to keep them more general. Over time, you'll learn what works best in your particular context.

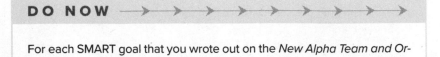

DO NOW

For each SMART goal that you wrote out on the *New Alpha Team and Organizational Planning Template*, list the relevant tasks in the third column.

Step 5. Note Any Other Tasks or To-Dos for the Year Ahead

Beyond listing the tasks that relate to each of your annual goals, don't forget to consider any other tasks or to-dos that might come up in the next year that you'll need to plan for.

Good examples of this kind of work are planning for board meetings, team retreats, and activities that support a successful group culture. These kinds of activities help to push the work forward, but they're not necessarily work activities that you'll naturally identify based on the annual goals that you identified in step 3.

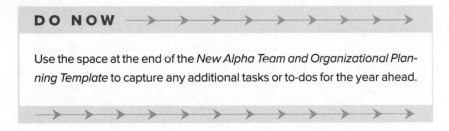

DO NOW

Use the space at the end of the *New Alpha Team and Organizational Planning Template* to capture any additional tasks or to-dos for the year ahead.

Step 6. Review your Fabulous Work

Once you've developed a well-fleshed-out plan, including anchors, priorities, goals, tasks, and to-dos, it's time to review your fabulous work!

DO NOW

Take a moment to address the following questions:

1. How have you incorporated your strategy and cultural priorities into this plan?

2. If you accomplish each of the annual goals in this document, where will you be one year from now in relation to the overall vision? Does each of the annual goals enable progress toward the vision? Are there any other goals that need to be changed or added? If so, do that now.

3. Do you have the resources (people, money, space, materials, equipment, and professional training and skills) to realistically accomplish each of these goals in the next year? Assign names and dollar amounts (and any other resources you can think of) to the major goals and tasks. Are there any work activities that need to be cut or deprioritized? If so, do that now.

4. What interdependencies do you see between various areas of the work for the next year? (For example, "Does my goal of developing a new public relations plan for the organization impact the folks who manage our website? What tasks does this project create for others who might not be on my team?") Communicate this information to others in your group as necessary.

We'll talk about how to communicate the plan more broadly in the next section, but for now, make sure that every single person involved in the planning process is aware of how the work that they're responsible for affects and is affected by the other portions of the plan.

COMMUNICATE THE PLAN

Communication leads to community—that is, to understanding, intimacy, and mutual valuing.
—ROLLO MAY, American existential psychologist

When you're confident that you have a solid plan in place, the next step is to communicate the plan broadly. At this point, if you're working on a large-scale plan and involving other people in the planning process, then these folks likely know the content of the plan. The question is: are there other members of the larger group who need to have this information as well? This includes anyone whose work is affected directly or indirectly by the work activities that are spelled out in the plan.

More specifically, everyone whom you're responsible for should be able to answer the following three questions:

1. What is the overarching vision for our team and organization's work? Where are we headed in the long term?

2. What is the plan to achieve the vision, and more specifically, how does my work and that of my team contribute to realizing the vision?

3. Which specific priorities, goals, tasks, and/or to-dos am I responsible for (or affected by) in the year ahead?

One of the best examples of an organization coming together to communicate the plan for the year ahead happened when I was working with the Carnegie Foundation. After we'd wrapped up the formal annual planning process, each team in the organization prepared a 10- to 15-minute presentation that described how the work that they were doing contributed to the larger vision.

As part of these presentations, each member of the team gave a brief description of how their specific roles and responsibilities contributed to the broader vision, and they announced any key projects that they "owned" in the year ahead and wanted to put on people's radar. Everyone cheered when our IT folks announced that they were preparing to give us the "fastest Internet in the world" so that we would have "the resources necessary to improve educational opportunities for students." It wasn't necessarily obvious how this group's work tied into the larger organizational vision, but they did an excellent job of making the connection.

As the official "leader" for one of these teams (Core Operations), I can say that our team put a lot of time and effort into developing this presentation, but it was well worth it. People within and outside of our team learned a lot, and the simple act of going through this activity forced each of us to get really clear on our roles and responsibilities and how these connected to the broader vision and the work ahead (which, of course, also made my job, as a leader, a lot easier in the long run).

If I could do this activity again, the only thing I would change would be to have had each team member create some "artifact" (maybe a sketch or diagram or statement) to capture the main takeaways from this activity.

This would have reinforced learning even after the presentations were over (while also fulfilling my by-now-obvious need to encourage creative expression wherever possible).

IDENTIFY THE RIGHT SUPPORT STRUCTURES FOR THE PLAN

The devil is in the details.
—Proverb

Once you've developed a plan and communicated it broadly, the final step in this phase is to make sure that you've identified the right support structures for the plan. You can do this by answering the following questions:

1. Given the work ahead, are there any team or organizational policies (overarching rules or guidelines) that you need to add or adjust to make the work happen as smoothly and efficiently as possible?

   For example, when I started working at Carnegie, we were in a period of intense and rapid growth. As many of the large projects began to take off, and more and more people needed to travel to meet with various partners in the field, we realized that some of our travel policies were overly restrictive and made employees' work more difficult to do. Based on their feedback, we adjusted these policies to be more supportive of how people actually worked.

2. What processes (series of actions or steps) or procedures (detailed, step-by-step instructions) are currently in place to support this work? Do you need to make any modifications or design any new ones?

   For example, what is the process for adjusting your annual plans when a new and unexpected work project comes up? Should the individuals responsible for the work simply figure out how to reprioritize their tasks, or do they need someone else's approval here? If so, who is the final "approver," and how does the approval process work? (Do you need to have a meeting, can the person approve over email, or something else?)

Thinking about these kinds of processes and procedures at the outset will reduce confusion, stress, and frustration for you and your team in the long run. (And as always, these aspects of your work are flexible, so you should expect to change and update them as the team and their work evolve.)

NEW ALPHA TEAM AND ORGANIZATIONAL PLANNING TEMPLATE

Priority	SMART Goal	Tasks

List any additional tasks or to-dos in the space below:

Figure 11.1 *New Alpha Team and Organizational Planning Template*

CHAPTER 12

Execute the Plan

Leadership is the capacity to translate vision into reality.
—WARREN BENNIS, American scholar,
organizational consultant, and author, widely regarded as a
pioneer of the contemporary field of leadership studies

When I was a junior in college, I was elected speaker of the Student
Government Association (SGA), a role that in conjunction with the
SGA vice president, nominated the chairpersons for each of the legislative
committees. That year, a transfer student named Eric was one of the people
who applied to chair the Governmental Affairs committee.

Since he was new to campus, we didn't know a lot about him, but
he was an obvious go-getter with an impressive list of big projects that
he'd already accomplished in his first month on campus. We decided to
nominate him for the role, and he was easily confirmed by the SGA's
legislative body.

In the weeks and months that followed, Eric quickly assembled the
rest of his committee. What's more, I noticed that each of these committee
members had clearly defined roles and specific tasks that they worked on,
and he met with them regularly to check progress and follow up. He was
also really good at *developing* them—encouraging them to take advantage
of experiences that would improve their performance on the committee
(and make them better leaders in the long run).

I remember being really impressed with how they worked as a group,
and particularly with Eric's leadership—and it wasn't just me who felt this
way. Countless SGA folks were always saying things like, "Eric and his

team really get things done. He's going to lead something big one day." Turns out, we were right. In 2013, Eric Swalwell became one of the youngest members elected to serve in the U.S. Congress, and you can bet that his ability to lead and manage others toward big goals was a key driver to his success.

As Eric's story demonstrates, more than just painting a compelling vision of the future and making a plan for how to get there, New Alpha leaders are able to work effectively with others to *execute* the plan. In this chapter, you'll learn what actions you can take to enliven the plan that you developed in the previous chapter.

UNDERSTAND WHAT YOUR PEOPLE DO

*The great gift of human beings is that
we have the power of empathy.*
—MERYL STREEP, American actress and
three-time Academy Award winner

One of the most common questions that I get asked is whether or not managers should be "experts" at the work of their team members. Believe it or not, the answer is no. As anyone who's ever worked for a technically competent, but bad manager will tell you, technical competence only goes so far.

It's nice if you have expertise in the areas of work that your team members are responsible for, but it's far more important that you're able to identify and communicate the vision, set priorities, clarify goals and tasks, procure resources, and help to clear obstacles.

With that said, you should absolutely do your best to understand the work that your team members do and to get yourself the training and support that you need in order to do this. This is basic empathy (see "Social Awareness" in Chapter 2, "Build Positive and Productive Relationships with Others"), and it will do wonders in terms of building trust and respect with the people you manage. It will also help you to make more informed decisions as a leader.

For example, when my friend and colleague, Jesse Noonan (now chief academic officer for the Youth Policy Institute), was hired as a school director for Teach For America's summer training program, she was ecstatic. The only problem was that her school director position centered on leading an elementary school team, and her teaching experience and expertise was with high school students and young adults.

Undaunted, Jesse accepted the role and then talked extensively with elementary teachers and administrators and observed their classrooms in order to better understand their work and the ways that it differed from her experiences with older students. As a result, she was a wildly successful school director and her team (and colleagues like me!) loved her.

The point is that you don't need to be an expert at every single aspect of your team's work. However, you should at least have a general understanding of what each person does and make an effort to fill any gaps.

SET AND CLARIFY EXPECTATIONS

Communicate with others as clearly as you can to avoid misunderstandings, sadness, and drama.
—MIGUEL ÁNGEL RUIZ, Mexican author

In the Vision and Plan phases of Part III, "Team and Organizational Leadership," you communicated the vision and plan to your team members. At this point, everyone on your team should be 100 percent clear on the *general roles and responsibilities for her or his position* and the *specific tasks and to-dos that she or he is responsible for in the year ahead*. (See "Help Your People Connect Their Work to the Vision" in Chapter 10, "Identify the Vision," for a recap of these conversations.)

If there is any confusion here, then have the conversation again. Be sure to update your team members if and when expectations change. Having this information will help your team members understand *why* certain projects get assigned to them and *what* they'll be working on for the next 12 months.

New Alpha Tip

Setting and clarifying expectations is particularly important if you're new to your leadership role and/or if you have a new team member who's less familiar with the group's vision and plan. (See *The New*

(continued)

Alpha Resource Guide for a meeting agenda template that you can use for your first meetings as a supervisor or with new team members.)

ASSIGN AND DELEGATE WORK WITH YOUR TEAM MEMBERS' *PERSONAL LEADERSHIP IDENTITIES* IN MIND

Whenever you can, give your team members projects and tasks that leverage their *Personal Leadership Identities*. This will help to sustain their engagement and motivation, and it will help you to strategically *delegate* your workload when you have more tasks on your plate than you can realistically accomplish.

When assigning work, don't forget to set *clear deadlines* and give your team members any *resources* (people, money, space, materials, equipment, and professional training or skills) that they might need. If you've done a good job of explaining both the vision and plan and connecting their role to the work, then the *why* of these projects and tasks should be obvious. If that's not the case, then do what you need to do to ensure that the team members are able to see how the assignment connects to the larger vision and plan. As is the case with organizational change, when people understand *why* they are being asked to do something, they're much more likely to embrace the assignment. (See "Model Transparency and Continuous Improvement" in Chapter 10, "Identify the Vision.")

Remember, unless a team member is new or having serious performance issues, don't tell him *how* to do his work. Your role as a leader and manager is to show him the big picture, to get him motivated and excited to get there, and then to unleash him to do it in the way that he sees fit. If you *micromanage* his work, by spelling out *how* he should be doing it, he will likely get bored and frustrated—and will eventually disengage.

With that said, if you notice that someone on your team is really struggling with a particular project or task, then by all means, offer to be a thought partner as she searches for appropriate solutions. Keep in mind, though, that the more you encourage her to come up with her own solutions, the less she will need to rely on you in the long run.

The key to effective people management is to strike the right balance between having your people struggle unnecessarily and having them over-rely on you to help get the job done.

CHECK PROGRESS AND FOLLOW UP

Quality is everyone's responsibility.
—W. Edwards Deming, American engineer,
statistician, and management consultant

Once you've laid the groundwork of the vision, plan, and expectations, and you've unleashed your team members to go do something incredible, you're all set, right?

Well, not exactly.

No matter how well you set people up for success or how high performing they are, you still need to check in with them regularly. Checking in helps to ensure that expectations and communications are clear and that each team member's work is coordinated with any other work that is going on within the larger group.

Your job as a manager is to bring out the best in your people, and regular check-ins give you opportunities to support your team members and help them to overcome any obstacles. Having regular "face time" with one another will also set the foundation for a strong working relationship, which will make your job easier in the long run.

You can check in with your team members in two ways: *informally*, for example, when you see them in the hallway, and *formally* through "regularly scheduled" formal check-ins.

How to Organize Your Formal Check-Ins

"Regularly scheduled" formal check-ins ensure that, no matter how busy or hectic things get, all of your team members have regular access to you, their leader, to discuss what's going on and to get support with prioritizing their work or overcoming any challenges or obstacles that they're facing.

Formal check-ins also help you to stay informed about your team's progress, so that you can make effective decisions about how to manage the work and delegate resources.

Here is how I suggest that you organize your check-in process with team members, based on what I've learned from the New Alphas who are exceptionally strong at people management:

- Talk with each team member and agree upon a regular day and time that you will check in. Feel free to adjust days, times, and frequencies to suit your needs, but be aware that leaving too much time in between check-ins with a team member can weaken internal communication over time.

- During each check-in, allot time for the team member to update you on his work, get help from you on anything that he is struggling with, share any new information that's relevant to the organization or his role, and to get answers from you to any questions that he might have.

- During your check-ins, you should be giving each team member positive feedback, which will help her recognize and leverage her skills and strengths. You should also be giving constructive feedback, which will help her further develop and improve her performance.

Many New Alpha leaders also schedule "extended check-ins" every three to six months with team members. You can use these sessions to have more in-depth conversations around areas of strength or recent "wins" as well as areas for growth and development. Check-ins and extended check-ins can also be a great way to get one-on-one feedback from your team members about what you can do to improve your own leadership and management capabilities.

In case it's helpful, I've included a sample check-in agenda, an extended check-in template, and a comprehensive list of growth and development opportunities for employees in *The New Alpha Resource Guide*.

A Note About Positive Feedback

You should absolutely give more positive than critical feedback. While the exact ratio is pretty hotly debated, most research suggests that at least three to four positive comments for every piece of critical feedback will lead to the best performance results.[1]

This doesn't mean that you want to avoid giving critical feedback at all, or that you should heap on the positive feedback as if there's no tomorrow. However, it does mean that you should be mindful of your ratio of positive to critical feedback. It also goes (almost!) without saying that any critical feedback that you give should be *constructive*; in other words: it should push the work forward. Critical feedback should never be perceived as complaining, malicious, sarcastic, or cynical.

Work on giving feedback in a way that's both honest and constructive. It takes practice, but you'll find that most people respond better and improve more quickly when you're constructive rather than negative with your critical feedback. In the long run, it also builds team member motivation and engagement.

Group Surveys

In addition to regular check-ins, you can get a read on the "pulse" of your group by administering group surveys. Some New Alpha leaders like to do this on a monthly basis, others quarterly or even yearly.

These surveys can be pretty informal (I recommend SurveyMonkey's free version), and you can use them to have people rate everything from the group culture, to the performance of group leaders, to the efficacy of staff meetings. You can also ask open-ended questions like, "What do you like best about [insert name of group here]?" and "How can we improve [insert name of group here]?"

They key to a successful group survey is to actually use the data, so that people know that it's worth their time to give thoughtful responses. The leaders who do this best share the results of the survey with the group (even if it doesn't paint a rosy picture of how things are going), and they communicate any changes or improvements that will be made based on the data. (See "Model Transparency and Continuous Improvement" in Chapter 10, "Identify the Vision.") In some cases, they may even ask the group for feedback and ideas based on the survey results.

Embracing this kind of radical group transparency can be scary, especially at first, but it's also the first step toward creating a shared understanding of what works well and what needs to be improved. Your courage and commitment to continuous improvement at this stage will earn buy-in and respect in the long run.

CONDUCT EFFECTIVE MEETINGS

*If you had to identify, in one word, the reason why the
human race has not achieved, and never will achieve, its full
potential, that word would be "meetings."*
—DAVE BARRY, Pulitzer Prize–winning
American author and columnist

Most people would do just about anything to avoid attending a meeting—
and this makes sense since most meetings are not an efficient use of time,
which can feel like the spiritual equivalent of gouging your eyeballs out
with a dull spoon. But there's good news. You can change all this by taking six simple actions:

1. **Appoint a meeting facilitator.** This person's role is to "manage" the
   meeting. This does not need to be you. Find someone with reasonably *strong emotional intelligence* who's good at corralling people
   and staying on time. Get people the training they need to do this,
   if necessary.

2. **Distribute an agenda prior to the meeting.** This should be done
   at least 24 hours in advance, and it should include items to be discussed, time estimates, and any prereading.

3. **Establish and enforce meeting norms.** These are similar to the
   cultural norms that your group has, but they relate specifically to
   how people should act during meetings. Write them down, post
   them before every meeting, and be a fanatic about reminding
   people to adhere to them.

4. **Stay on time and on task during the meeting.** Even if this makes
   people feel a little rushed, it teaches them to be efficient with their
   time. Plus, for most people, having a 30-minute meeting go on for
   60 or 90 minutes is equivalent to at least the fourth level of hell.

5. **Identify any decisions made and next steps.** Make sure you include *who exactly* is responsible for implementing any actions the
   groups agrees to take. In my experience, this step is one of the most

difficult to do because it involves lots of nitty-gritty details, which most people abhor, but it's also the most important because it forces people to be accountable for the work. *When this action doesn't happen, the meeting is often just a waste of everyone's time and energy.*

6. **Do a post-meeting evaluation.** At the end of the meeting, ask everyone to go around in a circle and give the meeting a rating (1 through 5, with 5 being the highest rating). Time permitting, ask everyone to share one thing that they like and appreciated about the meeting and one thing that they think would make the meeting even better next time. Track people's responses, and be sure to note any improvements that you've made based on their feedback at future meetings. (People love this!)

New Alpha Tip

If you're nervous that people won't feel comfortable giving the meeting an honest score, you can start by just asking everyone to give one piece of positive and one piece of constructive feedback on the meeting. Once they see that you use these data to improve future meetings, they'll get more comfortable in sharing actual number scores with the group.

DO NOW

Identify just one thing that, if changed, would make your meetings more efficient and effective:

Make a note to test this change in your next meeting—and if you are obsessed with good meetings (as I am!), check out the "Conduct Effective Meetings" section under Chapter 12 in *The New Alpha Resource Guide*.

CHAPTER

Sustaining Progress, Growth, and Motivation

The ability to apply the Vision-Plan-Execute process in a group is at the heart of effective team and organizational leadership. By now, you are well on your way to mastering this aspect of the New Alpha program. The ideas and activities outlined in this final chapter are designed to help you develop the competencies that you'll need to keep your group on track and engaged throughout the process.

COMMUNICATE, COMMUNICATE, AND COMMUNICATE SOME MORE

Keep Your Team Members Looped In

There's nothing more frustrating than working in a place where you have no clue what's going on. In these kinds of environments, it's easy for this frustration to fester over time and create resentment toward organizational and team leaders, while also fueling employee disengagement and decreased productivity.

To avoid this, whenever you receive new information that would be relevant to members of your team (for example, during meetings with senior leaders or someone in another department), make sure to share this info with your team. Information that should be shared includes updates to the organizational vision and plan, changes to company policy, new data about a competitor, or industry news. Whatever it is, just make sure you pass it along to the right people. When in doubt, over-communicate rather than under-communicate.

Also, don't forget that people will come to you, as a leader, with any questions that they have about the information that they're hearing. Be prepared for this, and think about how to communicate any difficult news in a way that's honest, empathetic, and not soul crushing.

New Alpha Tip

Develop a system for tracking the critical information that you need to share. For instance, I had a friend and colleague Rebecca Hartzler who kept a notebook that she carried around everywhere in order to keep track of exactly this type of information. Then at the end of each day, she went through and followed up as necessary—beautifully simple and efficient.

Here are some situations in which you can easily share information with team members:

- During team meetings

- At one-on-one check-ins

- When you walk around the building and see people

- At lunch (which you should be taking because breaks are important!)

- Via emails, text, or instant messages

- Through webinars, podcasts, or conference calls

- In group memos, newsletters, blogs, or a group project management tool (These usually work best as secondary forms of communication, after people have heard the information in person.)

I swear by all that is holy, keeping your team members looped in is probably the number one thing that will make your team love you. Speaking from personal experience, having the right information in a timely manner makes people feel respected, valued, engaged, and empowered to do their jobs well. Your team members will even forgive your occasional flubs if you just keep them looped in and connected.

DO NOW

Wherever you keep track of important information (a notebook, a Google Doc, or someplace else), create a space to note any important information that needs to be communicated to your team members. Capture critical communication in this space, and reiterate it to your team on a regular basis.

Keep the Organization Looped In

In addition to keeping your team looped in about new information that affects the organization, as a leader, it's your responsibility to *represent your team and their accomplishments to the organization.*

With this in mind, in a sincere and genuine way, be sure to talk up your team members and their accomplishments to your colleagues and supervisors. The objects of your bragging will be psyched when they hear it through the grapevine (and they'll be motivated to work all that much harder for you), and it will show your colleagues and other leaders how supportive and empowering you are.

ADMIT YOUR MISTAKES

Another question that I get asked a lot is whether you should admit your mistakes as a leader, or whether doing so makes you look weak. The answer is yes and maybe. Yes, when you make a mistake as a leader, the morally right thing to do is to acknowledge it. It's also true that this might make you *appear* weak or incompetent in the short run, but in the long run, it will underscore your courage and integrity, which will increase people's respect for you.

I've worked with and observed a number of leaders who've done this well and a few who've done it terribly. For those who do it well, the process generally involves six steps:

1. Acknowledge the mistake.

2. Apologize and take ownership of it.

3. Avoid blaming others.

4. Share what you've learned from this experience.

5. Identify any next steps to remedy the mistake and/or to avoid it in the future. (You might ask others to help you to generate options here.)

6. Move on and don't over-apologize or dwell on this mistake. (The people who end up looking "weak" for admitting mistakes are often those who forget or ignore this step.)

Keep in mind that everyone makes mistakes. What matters the most in good leadership is learning to deal with them in the most ethical and productive way possible.

CHAMPION INNOVATION AND CONTINUOUS IMPROVEMENT

Truly exceptional leaders and managers go beyond just achieving the agreed upon goals. They consistently encourage new and better ways of doing the work. Whether this entails brainstorming new processes, developing new products, or completely overhauling how you work together, create space for your people to use their imaginations, and be sure to point out and praise innovation and improvement when you see it.

You can do this by engaging in a nonjudgmental, anything-goes "flaring" session before getting into the details of the work, or by giving your team members opportunities for training and development in creativity and design thinking, or even just by giving people time and space away from their regular work to think creatively. Carnegie was especially great at this last one. My colleagues often had jigsaw puzzles and board games in their offices, and we engaged in the occasional 3 p.m. group dance party for no reason other than to step away from the work and focus our brains elsewhere.

Giving people opportunities and space to think creatively and make the work better will increase their motivation and engagement—and support a successful group culture. This is particularly true for people who may be feeling frustrated or disengaged. In these cases, it's a good idea to encourage these folks to voice their concerns. But also, be sure to empower *them* to make changes. Don't think that you need to be everybody's savior. Empowering them will help them increase their problem-solving abilities *and* will save you time and effort in the long run because you won't be the only person in the group trying to think up and implement new ideas and improvements.

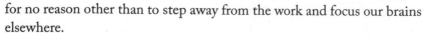

DO NOW

In what ways is your team innovative and improvement-focused? What specific actions can you take to support this type of mindset? What can you do to encourage this behavior from your group? Jot your ideas down here:

RESOLVE INTERPERSONAL CONFLICTS

No matter how effective you are as a leader and manager, conflicts between team members are inevitable. And such conflicts can even be positive developments if they ultimately push the work forward without damaging group culture and relationships in the process.

As a leader and manager, you're likely to either experience an interpersonal conflict or be required to help resolve a conflict between others. While most experts agree that there's no one single best way to manage conflict,[1] I've found that the following process generally produces positive and productive outcomes and is based heavily in the competencies

that you developed in the "Developing Emotional Intelligence" section of Chapter 2, "Build Positive and Productive Relationships with Others":

- Arrange a time and place where you can meet privately with the parties involved. Ideally, get this on everyone's calendars as soon as possible to prevent a situation in which one of the parties has more information than another about next steps.

- When you meet with the parties involved, set ground rules: no interrupting and stay focused on specific behaviors rather than generalizations or accusations.

- Give each party the opportunity to share their perspective about what's going on. While they do this, the other party should not interrupt.

- After each party speaks, ask the other party to restate what they think they heard. The point here is not to argue but to ensure that each party clearly understands the other party's perspective. Encourage the parties to ask questions if they are confused about anything that the other is saying.

- Allow as much time as you think is necessary to get all of the relevant issues out on the table.

- During this time, you might take notes on a notepad or white board, but be sure that you're engaged enough to enforce the ground rules.

- Check for understanding. Restate what you see as the major points of conflict.

- Allow the parties to adjust and tweak your restatements, if necessary.

- If appropriate, it can be helpful to note any points of agreement that you see at this stage.

- If there are many points of conflict, help the parties to prioritize the top two or three to focus on.

- Have the parties generate a list of possible solutions. Unless it becomes necessary, try not to feed them solutions. They'll be more motivated and empowered to actually follow through if they have the opportunity to generate the solutions on their own. Give them some time to think about this and write down all the options.

- Ask the parties to identify the option that they believe is most likely to lead to an optimal outcome. (If you've followed the previous steps in their entirety, this shouldn't be that hard to do. If you haven't, then this step will be tricky to manage, and it may involve your having to choose one for them—which will move things along but may also decrease their buy-in to the final decision.)

- Schedule individual or group follow-up sessions as necessary. This last part of the process is critical! Even if the parties come to what you believe is a workable outcome, you must follow up to make sure that the solution to which the parties agreed is being implemented. If you fail to take this step, the conflict may rage on and will likely get worse while continuing to suck up your time and energy.

In the spirit of the old proverb "Teach a person to fish, and she'll eat for a lifetime," remember that your goal as a manager is not necessarily to resolve every conflict as quickly and efficiently as possible. Instead, your role is to *facilitate* an exchange that will ultimately help the people involved learn to resolve their conflicts without your involvement.

MAKE GOOD AND TIMELY DECISIONS

In any moment of decision, the best thing you can do
is the right thing, the next best thing is the wrong thing,
and the worst thing you can do is nothing.
—THEODORE ROOSEVELT, American statesperson,
author, explorer, soldier, naturalist, and reformer who served as
the twenty-sixth president of the United States

One of your most important responsibilities as a leader is to make good decisions in a timely manner. This is another one of those competencies that sounds obvious but that many people (myself included!) often struggle with. Either we're too impulsive and make split-second decisions about things that we actually need to think more about, or we're overachiever-perfectionists who live in fear of making the wrong decision, and thus we delay decision making for as long as possible.

Both of these situations are a problem if you want to advance to a senior leadership position because these types of roles generally require the ability to make good and timely decisions on a fairly regular basis. Not to worry though. There is a fairly simple process that you can follow that will help you to optimize your ability to make good decisions under pressure:

- **Gather and analyze facts and background information.** What is the decision that needs to be made? What are the overarching goals that relate to this decision? What do you already know? Be sure to ask any questions that you have.

- **Identify any past experiences or frameworks that you know of that might be relevant to this situation or context.** Are there any other people whose counsel you should seek out? If time permits, reach out to them.

- **Identify all of the possible options.**

- **Analyze the possible pros and cons for each option.** Be sure to consider how each option affects the relevant goals that you've identified *and* the people involved.

- **Make a decision.** Given the information that you have, which decision option is most likely to lead to the best possible outcome in the long term?

- **Implement the decision, and reflect on what went well and what needs to be improved.** Possible improvements might relate to the decision itself or to your decision-making process.

While this process isn't a magic bullet that will guarantee perfect results every time, following it will help you find the right balance of decision quality and decision timeliness.

MANAGE UP

Just as you need to clarify the vision and strategy for the people who report to you, make sure that you do the same with your managers. If your manager asks you to do something, be sure you know what it means to do the project or task well, including any relevant deadlines.

While you might think that this would drive managers nuts (and I suppose it could if you were super overzealous about it . . .), most of them really appreciate it when you clarify expectations at the outset. Also, don't be afraid to follow up to ask any necessary questions, to let her know that you've completed the task, or to remind her to do something that she agreed to. If the latter, be polite about it, but don't avoid following up just so that you don't offend her. If she happens to get offended, then it's probably more her issue than yours.

DO NOW → → → → → → → → →

What expectations around your organization's vision and goals, or your role, are still somewhat hazy to you? Do you know what is expected of you and by when? Do you know what your next position or role within the organization might be, and how you can work toward it?

If your answer is no to either of those last two questions, make an appointment with your supervisor to have a low-key and gracious conversation in order to get clarity. If you do this well, you'll not only gain the information that you need to be successful and to advance in your career but you'll also show your supervisor that you're engaged in the work and committed to taking your impact to the next level. Unless your supervisor is an insecure jerk, he'll appreciate your initiative here.

→ → → → → → → → → → → →

SUPPORT GROWTH AND DEVELOPMENT

One of the key functions of a leader and manager is to support growth and development opportunities for people. This includes helping your team members identify appropriate training opportunities to increase their technical skills *and* their leadership competencies.

Not everyone on your team is going to come perfectly packaged as the best version of themselves, but New Alpha leaders and managers know how to develop people to their full potential—for their current role and beyond. This, in turn, helps the group to achieve its goals, keeps people engaged and excited about their next steps, and helps to cultivate the rising generation of leaders for your team and organization.

DO NOW →→ → →→ →→ →→ →→ →→→

Ask each of your team members to complete the *New Alpha Professional Development Plan* in Table 13.1 before your next check-in. (A download-able copy of this form is available at www.LeadershipAndHumanPotential.com/Resources.) When you meet with them, discuss what they included, provide any feedback about what you see as particularly important (especially around their growth as a leader), and secure agreement around next steps.

Table 13.1 **New Alpha Professional Development Plan**

Where Do You Want to Be in 1 Year? 5 Years? 10 or More Years?	What Knowledge, Skills, or Aspects of Your Personality Do You Need to Develop in Order to Advance?	What Actions Can You Take to Increase Your Competency in These Areas?	Identify Specific Next Steps and Expected Completion Dates.

For all of the reasons that your team members need growth and development plans, you should also have your own growth and development plan. This will help you make good long-term decisions and stay focused on next steps as you advance in your career.

DO NOW ➤ ➤ ➤ ➤ ➤ ➤ ➤ ➤ ➤

Review your personal vision board and *Personal Leadership Identity Statement* and *One-Pager*. Then complete the *New Apha Professional Development Plan* in Table 13.1 for yourself. When you've completed it, make an appointment to speak with your manager or supervisor about your long-term goals and development. Be sure to ask her for specific feedback about your goals, including any specific next steps. Also, remember to mention the information from this document every so often (every three to four months or so), so that it stays on this person's radar.

➤ ➤ ➤ ➤ ➤ ➤ ➤ ➤ ➤ ➤ ➤

CONNECT EVERYTHING BACK TO THE VISION

The most basic truth about effective leadership is that everything you do or say as a leader should support and tie back to the larger vision. Every aspect of the culture that you build, every plan that you make, every goal that you set, every meeting that you hold, every piece of feedback that you give, every decision that you make ... every single action that you take as a leader should influence and motivate your people toward the larger vision.

Take a close look at the way that you spend your time and how you interact with your colleagues, and ruthlessly cut everything that doesn't directly or indirectly support the vision. Also, think about additional actions that you can take going forward to better support the vision.

DO NOW

Think back to the past week. List everything that you remember working on or spending time on—from the items on your daily schedule to informal conversations that you had with colleagues:

Now, circle any items that don't tie back to, or support, the larger vision. How can you eliminate these kinds of activities going forward?

Finally, make a list of the activities that you don't currently do, but that you could do, in order to better connect your work, and the work of your team, to the larger vision:

Well done! You've now officially completed Part III, "Team and Organizational Leadership."

Congratulations and
Advice for the Road

Be patient toward all that is unsolved in your heart,
and try to love the questions themselves like locked rooms
and like books that are written in a foreign tongue.
—Rainer Maria Rilke,
Bohemian-Austrian poet and novelist

Dear Reader,

Congratulations! If you've made it this far and you've completed all of the self-assessments and learning and reflection activities along the way, then I have no doubt that you are well on your way to being a New Alpha leader and doing all of the great things in this world that only you—with your particular combination of talents and gifts—can do.

A word of guidance before you put down this book: whether you're an experienced leader or just starting out on your leadership journey, expect to struggle (sometimes repeatedly) as you work toward your vision. As South African President Nelson Mandela wrote in his autobiography: "After climbing a great hill, one only finds that there are many more hills to climb." Anticipate experiencing fear, anxiety, and even disappointment. And know that, whether you embrace them or not, they are an essential part of your development, and ultimately, your path to New Alpha leadership.

As you make your way along this path, also keep in mind that, at its core, New Alpha leadership is often a careful balancing act. For instance, you may find yourself wondering how to be *proactive* without stepping on toes (*relationship management*) or wondering about exactly how kind and generous you should be to someone who clearly doesn't respect you as a human being. These aren't just tough questions for you. They're tough questions for all of us, and in the end, each individual must find the right balance that works for her or him as an individual. However, if you've spent time really digging into the ideas and competencies outlined in this book (and even rereading entire sections and chapters when you need to), then over time, you'll get better at making the choices that create the right balance for *you*. I've also found that in those moments of feeling overwhelmed, confused, or scared, the best course of action can always be found in our answer to the following question: *which course of action creates more joy and/or less suffering in the world?* Stick with this approach, and you'll eventually find your way.

And remember to be kind to yourself. It's so easy to fall into the perfectionist trap of not taking risks in order to avoid failure, but in the end, this doesn't usually take us anywhere interesting or meaningful in life. Instead, open yourself up to the adventure that lies ahead, and measure your success, not against some flawless ideal or against what others are doing, but in terms of your own continuous learning and progress. Celebrate your wins, maybe even your failures, too, and treat yourself as you believe the person who loves you most in this world would treat you: with kindness and encouragement.

Also, remember to share the New Alpha approach with others, including friends, family, colleagues, and other leaders. This will help them to grow and improve, and the process of sharing this information will reinforce your own learning and development. Getting the word out will also help us on our shared mission to redefine leadership for the modern world.

To this end, remember that you're not alone. All across the globe there are others of us working to ignite significant and lasting change in our lives, our organizations, and the world, and we're grateful for your role in this movement.

Thank you, and carpe diem!
Danielle

For additional support and resources, or to share your stories,
we invite you to keep in touch via our newsletter
(www.LeadershipAndHumanPotential.com/Newsletter)
and by joining the conversation on social media.

Notes

CHAPTER 1

1. Z. Franco and P. Zimbardo, "The Banality of Heroism," September 1, 2006, retrieved December 18, 2014, from http://greatergood.berkeley.edu/article/item/the_banality _of_heroism.
2. Stephen Covey, A. Roger Merrill, and Rebecca R. Merrill, *First Things First: To Live, to Love, to Learn, to Leave a Legacy*, Simon & Schuster, New York, 1994.

CHAPTER 2

1. Don't believe me? Check this out: R. Cross, "Of Pies and Cars," *Big Sur Tales*, Author House, Bloomington, IN, 2010, p. 68.
2. C. Cherniss and D. Goleman, *The Emotionally Intelligent Workplace: How to Select for, Measure, and Improve Emotional Intelligence in Individuals, Groups, and Organizations*, Jossey-Bass, San Francisco, 2001.
3. D. Goleman, R. E. Boyatzis, and A. McKee, *Primal Leadership: Unleashing the Power of Emotional Intelligence*, Harvard Business Review Press, Boston, 2013.
4. D. Goleman, (1998). "What Makes a Leader?" *Harvard Business Review*, vol. 76, no. 6, pp. 93–102.
5. A. M. Grant, *Give and Take: A Revolutionary Approach to Success*, Viking, New York, 2013.
6. K. A. Case, J. Iuzzini, and M. Hopkins, (2012). "Systems of Privilege: Intersections, Awareness, and Applications," *Journal of Social Issues*, vol. 68, no. 1, pp. 1–10.
7. Kimberle Crenshaw, (1989-01-01). "Demarginalizing the Intersection of Race and Sex: A Black Feminist Critique of Antidiscrimination Doctrine, Feminist Theory and Antiracist Politics," *University of Chicago Legal Forum*, vol. 140, pp. 139–167; and Susanne V. Knudsen, "Intersectionality: A Theoretical Inspiration in the Analysis of Minority Cultures and Identities in Textbooks," in Éric Bruillard, Mike Horsley, Bente Aamotsbakken, et al., "Caught in the Web or Lost in the Textbook," *Proceedings of the 8th International Association for Research on Textbooks and Educational Media (IARTEM) Conference on Learning and Educational Media*, held in Caen, October 2005, IARTEM, Utrecht, the Netherlands, 2006, pp. 61–76.
8. A. G. Johnson, *Privilege, Power, and Difference*, McGraw-Hill, Boston, 2006.
9. "With great power comes great responsibility," retrieved July 23, 2015, from http://quoteinvestigator.com/2015/07/23/great-power/.

CHAPTER 3

1. • "Healthy Eating Plan," National Heart, Lung, and Blood Institute, no date, retrieved August 22, 2014, from https://www.nhlbi.nih.gov/health/educational /lose_wt/eat/calories.htm.

- L. K. Heilbronn et al., "Effect of 6-Month Calorie Restriction on Biomarkers of Longevity, Metabolic Adaptation, and Oxidative Stress in Overweight Individuals: A Randomized Controlled Trial," *Journal of the American Medical Association*, vol. 295, no. 13, 2006, pp. 1539–1548.
- "Is Eating Between Meals Good for Our Health?" European Food Information Council, no date, retrieved August 19, 2014, from http://www.eufic.org/article/en /expid/review-eating-between-meals-health/.
- D. J. Jenkins, P. Corey, T. M. Wolever, R. G. Josse, W. Singer, and R. Patten, et al., "Nibbling Versus Gorging: Metabolic Advantages of Increased Meal Frequency," *New England Journal of Medicine*, vol. 321, no. 14, 1989, pp. 929–934.
- J. E. Loehr, and T. Schwartz, *The Power of Full Engagement: Managing Energy, Not Time, Is the Key to High Performance and Personal Renewal*, Free Press, New York, 2003. (Note: This finding is not well substantiated by empirical research—but I'm including it anyway because in my personal experience, it's true.)
- Y. Ma, E. R. Bertone, E. J. Stanek III, G. W. Reed, J. R. Hebert, N. L. Cohen, et al., "Association Between Eating Patterns and Obesity in a Free-Living U.S. Adult Population," *American Journal of Epidemiology*, vol. 158, no. 1, 2003, pp. 85–92.
- W. C. Miller, D. M. Koceja, and E. J. Hamilton, "A Meta-analysis of the Past 25 Years of Weight Loss Research Using Diet, Exercise or Diet Plus Exercise Intervention," *International Journal of Obesity*, vol. 21, no. 10, 1997, pp. 941–947.
- "Nutrition and Healthy Eating," Mayo Clinic, no date, retrieved August 18, 2014, from http://www.mayoclinic.org/healthy-living/nutrition-and-healthy-eating /basics/nutrition-basics/hlv-20049477.
- M. Stevens, "Healthy Eating on the Go," Cleveland Clinic, no date, retrieved August 19, 2014, from http://my.clevelandclinic.org/heart/prevention/nutrition /food-choices/healthy-eating-on-the-go.aspx.

2. According to the Mayo Clinic, this means about 200 to 330 milligrams of caffeine per day (or about two to four cups of coffee). See "How Much Water Should You Drink Every Day?" *WebMD*, no date, retrieved August 17, 2014, from http://www .webmd.com/a-to-z-guides/drinking-enough-water-topic-overview.

3. "Sleep Deprivation Effects and How Much Sleep We Need: Babies, Teens, and Adults," *WebMD*, no date, retrieved August 21, 2014, from http://www.webmd.com /sleep-disorders/guide/sleep-requirements; and White Paper: *How Much Sleep Do Adults Need?* no date, retrieved August 21, 2014, from http://sleepfoundation.org /sleep-polls-data/white-papers/how-much-sleep-do-adults-need/page/0%2C6/.

4. B. Fryer, "Sleep Deficit: The Performance Killer," *Harvard Business Review*, October 2006, retrieved August 17, 2014, from http://hbr.org/2006/10/sleep-deficit-the -performance-killer/ar/1#.

5. "Exercise: 7 Benefits of Regular Physical Activity," February 5, 2014, retrieved from http://www.mayoclinic.org/healthy-living/fitness/in-depth/exercise/art-20048389 and "Staying Active," no date, retrieved from https://www.hsph.harvard.edu /nutritionsource/staying-active/ and M. Hitti, "Exercise May Boost Performance on the Job," *WebMD*, June 8, 2005, retrieved from http://www.webmd.com/fitness -exercise/20050608/exercise-may-boost-performance-on-job and "7 Ways You Can Easily Increase Your Willpower," no date, retrieved from http://www.bakadesuyo .com/2014/07/willpower/.

6. 2008 Physical Activity Guidelines for Americans [PDF]. (2008, October). U.S. Department of Health and Human Services.

7. R. F. Baumeister, K. D. Vohs, and D. M. Tice, (2007). "The Strength Model of Self-Control." *Current Directions in Psychological Science*, vol. 16, no. 6, pp. 351–355.

8. J. Segal, M. Smith, R. Segal, and L. Robinson, "Stress Symptoms, Signs, and Causes," no date, retrieved from http://www.helpguide.org/articles/stress/stress-symptoms -causes-and-effects.htm.

CHAPTER 4

1. A. L. Duckworth, C. Peterson, M. D. Matthews, and D. R. Kelly, "Grit: Perseverance and Passion for Long-Term Goals," *Journal of Personality and Social Psychology*, vol. 92, no. 6, 2007, pp. 1087–1101.

2. *IBM 2010 Global CEO Study: Creativity Selected as Most Crucial Factor for Future Success*, May 18, 2010, retrieved from http://www-03.ibm.com/press/us/en /pressrelease/31670.wss.

3. S. B. Kaufman, "Which Character Strengths Are Most Predictive of Well-Being?" *Scientific American*, no date, retrieved from http://blogs.scientificamerican.com /beautiful-minds/which-character-strengths-are-most-predictive-of-well-being/.

CHAPTER 5

1. J. Bolker, *Writing Your Dissertation in Fifteen Minutes a Day: A Guide to Starting, Revising, and Finishing Your Doctoral Thesis*, Henry Holt, New York, 1998.

2. Contrary to the popular belief that new habits take about 21 days to form, in actuality, a new habit takes, on average, just over two months to take hold, but that timing can vary depending on the person, frequency of behavior, and so on. See P. Lally, C. H. Jaarsveld, H. W. Potts, and J. Wardle, "How Are Habits Formed: Modelling Habit Formation in the Real World," *European Journal of Social Psychology*, vol. 40, no. 6, 2009, pp. 998–1009.

3. L. B. Clausen, Clayman Institute for Gender Research, November 18, 2013, retrieved from http://gender.stanford.edu/news/2013/multipliers-are-key-rethinking -time.

4. A. Grant and S. Sandberg, "Madam C.E.O., Get Me a Coffee," February 6, 2015, retrieved from http://www.nytimes.com/2015/02/08/opinion/sunday/sheryl -sandberg-and-adam-grant-on-women-doing-office-housework.html?_r=0.

5. D. Lloyd and E. L. Rossi, *Ultradian Rhythms in Life Processes: An Inquiry into Fundamental Principles of Chronobiology and Psychobiology*, Springer-Verlag, London, 1992.

6. Said to Samuel J Woolf, Berlin, summer 1929. Cited with additional notes in *The Ultimate Quotable Einstein* by Alice Calaprice and Freeman Dyson, Princeton University Press, Princeton, NJ, 2010, p. 230.

7. M. Oppezzo and D. L. Schwartz, "Give Your Ideas Some Legs: The Positive Effect of Walking on Creative Thinking," *Journal of Experimental Psychology: Learning, Memory, and Cognition*, vol. 40, no. 4, 2014, pp. 1142–1152.

8. R. Babineaux and J. D. Krumboltz, *Fail Fast, Fail Often: How Losing Can Help You Win*, TarcherPerigee, New York, 2013.

CHAPTER 7

1. Mary Oliver, "The Summer Day," *New and Selected Poems*, Beacon Press, Boston, 1992.

2. G. E. Vaillant, *Spiritual Evolution: A Scientific Defense of Faith*, New York: Broadway Books, New York, 2008.

CHAPTER 9

1. K. A. Case, J. Iuzzini, and M. Hopkins, "Systems of Privilege: Intersections, Awareness, and Applications," *Journal of Social Issues*, vol. 68, no. 1, 2012, pp. 1–10.

CHAPTER 10

1. B. D. Rosso, K. H. Dekas, and A. Wrzesniewski, "On the Meaning of Work: A Theoretical Integration and Review," *Research in Organizational Behavior*, vol. 31, 2011, pp. 91–127.

CHAPTER 12

1. B. L. Fredrickson, "Updated Thinking on Positivity Ratios," *American Psychologist*, vol. 68, no. 9, 2013, pp. 814–822.

CHAPTER 13

1. M. A. Rahim, "Toward a Theory of Managing Organizational Conflict," *International Journal of Conflict Management*, vol. 13, no. 3, 2002, pp. 206–235.

Acknowledgments

always tell people that I have the best job ever: I get to study exceptional people and share what I learn. And while discussing this idea with a colleague a few weeks ago, he observed, "It seems like you have some sort of skill for finding these people and getting them to dissect their magic with you," and I think that's basically right. Whatever flaws I may have (of which, I can assure you, there are many), I'm really good at finding exceptional people to learn from and then sharing their tips, tricks, and tools with others. (And doing so is definitely part of my *Personal Leadership Identity*.) So, in the spirit of this observation, I want to close this book with appreciation for all of the many outstanding people who've influenced and shaped the ideas in this book.

My first thanks go to my fabulous agent, Lisa Hagan, and world-class editor at McGraw-Hill, Cheryl Ringer. From the first time I tried to match us with characters from Harry Potter (and realized that I am, truly, Neville Longbottom) to the many, many *Stepbrothers* references that were shared, working with you two was both educational and hilarious! I'm thankful for the chance that you both were willing to take on this project (and on me!) and for the boundless energy, incredible talent, and immense fun that you brought to the writing and publishing process. I feel lucky to work with you both and luckier still to call you my friends. Cheryl, I'm also grateful that you connected me with rock stars like Chelsea Van der Gaag, Mauna Eichner, Lee Fukui, Marci Nugent, Richard Surmacz, Ann Pryor, Pattie Amoroso, Lisa Schweickert, Mark Trosino, and Jeff Weeks—and all of the other incredibly talented folks at McGraw-Hill who worked tirelessly to bring the New Alpha vision to life.

People often ask me how I came to study New Alpha leaders, and my answer is always the same: it started with the extraordinary student leaders that I met at the University of Maryland College Park (a number of whom are mentioned in this book). Big thanks in particular to Jamila Hall, James Bond, Angela Cabellon, Laron Hines, Mark Tervakoski, Darren Schneider,

Melanie Medina, Eric Swalwell, Stuart McPhail, Adia Moore, Steve Grimes, Ahnna Smith, Patrick Wu, Stacey Schwaber, Malav Patel, (Gene) Patrick Smith, and Christina Braganza. Thanks also to Krista Werbeck, Mia Moran, Katie Kaibni, Colleen O'Brien, and Rachel Lovelady, who reminded me of the importance of friendship and laughter—and not taking myself too seriously. Malaika Serrano and Kara Smith—it took me a few years after graduation to connect with you two, but I'm so glad that I did, and I am grateful for the wisdom and insights that you both shared in reviewing parts of the preliminary manuscript for this book. Jeanne Hart-Steffes and Wayne McIntosh: thank you for introducing me to what mentorship *should* look like in higher education.

The educators and education advocates whom I've worked with over the course of my career have also had a distinctive impact on my perspectives on leadership, and many of these folks came from Teach For America. In particular, I want to thank Leena Im, Jessica Bolhouse, Sean Waldheim, Pablo DePaz, Shannon Leonard, Kermit Cook, Nick Chan, Dena Kimball, Laura Feeney, Kathy Ray, Alison Banks, Maureen Ferry, Beth Napleton, Lynni Nordheim, Rob Strain, Kristen Duprel, Rachel Brainerd, Eric Acosta-Verprauskus, Katherine Acosta-Verprauskus, and Alexandra Bissonnette. Also Rachel Mendoza, Arlene Illa, and Marcella Fehely—thanks for molding me into a better teacher, a better leader, and a better person. To Jesse Noonan, Melissa Avila, Marianna Hennig, and Melanie Gleason—thanks especially for the ongoing support, empathy, and friendship (and to Jesse and Melanie for being early readers and commenters on parts of this manuscript).

To my friends who work or previously worked at the American Civil Liberties Union of the Nation's Capital: thanks for continuing to remind me that there are still people who are willing to forgo big salaries and fancy offices to be a force for good in the world. Art Spitzer, Johnny Barnes, and Don Haines—knowing you has changed me for the better. Kate Epstein—there is no one I'd rather traipse around D.C. with, on an impossible research mission, than you. (I believe that I also still owe you a dog-sitting.)

To the folks I met at Stanford University: thank you for helping me realize that it is absolutely possible to do what people say is impossible—and for making my brain a whole lot smarter in the process. In particular, I want to thank David Brady, Rob Reich, and Mo Fiorina for the support, kindness, and patience that you've shown me over the years (and to David, in particular, for letting me use you as an example in some of my public talks, which reminds me that I should tell you: I sometimes use you as an example in my public talks . . .). Also, Paul Gowder, Aila Matanock, Rachel Brulé, Rachel Stein, Sarah Anzia, Molly Cohn Jackman, Saul Jackman, Amanda Greene, Tresha Francis Ward, Lambrina Kless, Alexis Patterson, Cecilia Mo, Vardaan Chawla, and Belinda Chiang—I learned so much from each of you and treasure your friendship, however far apart we may be. Jackie Sargent, Eliana Vasquez, and Chandelle Arambula—you three make stuff happen and I'm grateful that I got to improve my skills by watching you in action. Finally, Kim Meredith, Tom Schnaubelt, Vivian Brates, and Milbrey McLaughlin—thank you for the mentorship, friendship, and occasional coffee (or wine!) breaks.

To the folks at Global Leadership Adventures (Terra Education)— as soon as I met Andrew Motiwalla, I knew that GLA was going to be an awesome and life-changing experience. From climbing mountains in the rain with Annabel Smith (and being moved to tears by just about every one of her talks . . .), to eating friend food on the side of the road with Jessica Rose Miller at 1 a.m., to forcing Richard Bourlet to do aerobics on a semi-regular basis in Costa Rica, I'm so grateful for the experience of having worked with such insightful, conscientious, and wildly fun people— and for the lifelong friendships (and comical gaiety!) that has followed.

Also, as I've pretty much told anyone who asks: working at the Carnegie Foundation was a hugely positive and life-changing experience. In particular, I'm grateful to Tony Bryk for always believing in me. To the operations team, and especially Trinh Kabbabe, Doug Mihok, Jonathan Benjamin, Charlene Moran, Anne Betts, and Steve Giusti—you all exemplify the idea that it pays to build a team of people who are better than you. (Haha—I only wish I could take credit for hiring all of you!) You made leading our Core Ops team a privilege and a pleasure. Sola Takahashi, Jeannie Myung, Bernadine Fong, Miguel Socias, Heidi Pio, Gay Clyburn, Penny Carver, Jane Muhich, Lawrence Morales, Rebecca Hartzler, Nisha Patel, Elena Silva, Taylor White, Eva Mejia, Kim Gomez, Corey Donahue, Cinnamon Hillyard, Natalie Bold, Mike Smith, Amelia Belch, Rehaan Jahanghir, Rachel Mudge, Nicole Gray, Amaya Webster, Holly Szafarek, Krissia Martinez, Lillian Kivel, Allie Stone, Susan Headden, Hannah Hausman, and Peter Jung—aside from the fact that you all made Carnegie an organization that was the perfect combination of wicked smart and impactful, it was also a ton of fun! From our Drop Everything And Dance

(DEAD) parties, to our overly competitive scavenger hunts, to that time we successfully pressured Tony to use "theme music" during his report to the board—I learned so much! Moreover, every single one of you influenced me in some important way, and I continue to value your presence in my life. Dania Frink—thanks especially for lending your artistic and design expertise when I needed it. One more thing: Louis Gomez—you are possibly the most flawless human being I've ever met ... except for your taste in fiction.

In addition to all of the aforementioned great folks, I'm also incredibly lucky and blessed to have learned from excellent mentors like Carrie Coltman (one of the most creative minds I've ever met), Cathy Casserly (one of the few instances where you meet someone who is "legendary" and she or he is *even better* in person), Vera Bennett (who graciously shared all of her operations expertise with me during my time at Carnegie), Anna Waring (who constantly reminds me to do the most good that I can with my time here on earth), and Ashley Franks (who showed me that *mentees* can also make superb *mentors*). Julie Lythcott-Haims—you are just pure goodness; thank you for taking me under your wing and sharing the magic.

I'm also grateful to Melissa Collison Hendricks, John Collins, Alison Taylor Jayne, Amritha Subramanian, Shana Levine, and Sara Collison— lifelong friends who cheered me on when I was ahead, shared the *best* advice, and also helped to pick me up after the big failures. Gail Chambers— having you as a teacher changed my life. To the Palo Alto Lean In group and my fabulous writing group (you know who you are)—thank you for the friendship and inclusiveness that you've shown me since I launched the Center for Advancing Leadership and Human Potential. Also, Danielle Wohl, Bob Baxley, Heather Kirkpatrick, Carolyn Brady, Andy Petranek, Reb Rebele, Adam Grant, Tom Kolditz, Sally Thornton, Josh Becker, Anne Loehr, Casey Gerald, Ellen Cassidy, Faith Lin, and Neetal Parekh: thanks for being early and enthusiastic contributors and ideators to, and supporters of, this project, in particular. To the students in my courses at Stanford and Berkeley—I'm so grateful for the energy and creativity that you brought to our group, and it's no surprise that many of the ideas and topics covered in this book came directly from conversations that we had.

To Aaron Grayson, Anna Kawar, Chand John, Chantal Laurie Below, and Steve Kaagan (who also reviewed early portions of the manuscript)— thanks for the energy, ideas, and brainpower that you bring to our work at the Center for Advancing Leadership and Human Potential and for being a part of this journey.

And finally, my family, most of all, deserves my biggest thanks. Mom and Dad—thanks for teaching me the stuff that matters most: kindness, empathy, helping others, and love, love, love. Like any good millennial, I pretty much thank my lucky stars every day that I got you two for parents. Kenny, Rosa, Grandma Betty, Grandma Ruth, Dona, Connie, Bree, Aaron, Justin, Jeremy, and Jules—thanks for the ongoing love and support (and all of the constructive debate . . . and occasional food fights). To the Warrens (and especially Naomi Petrash, who painstakingly edited *and* copyedited the original 77-page book proposal for this book)—thanks for the never-ending enthusiasm and encouragement. And to Nick Warren, my partner, best friend, coconspirator, and great love: I treasure your presence in my life and am in constant awe of your kindness, integrity, and creative vision. Thank you for making me laugh hard every day and feel the kind of joy that I hadn't felt since I was a kid.

Index

About the Author

Danielle Harlan is the founder and CEO of the Center for Advancing Leadership and Human Potential. She earned her doctorate in political science and her master's in education from Stanford University, where she was a Jacob K. Javits National Fellow and received a Centennial Teaching Award for excellence in instruction. Prior to launching the Center, she was the chief of operations for the Carnegie Foundation, where she worked to harness the power of networks and quality improvement strategies in order to solve important educational problems.

Named one of Silicon Valley's "40 Under 40," Danielle has also been a speaker for TEDx, and she has worked as an instructor at the Stanford Graduate School of Business and UC Berkeley Extension's Corporate and Professional Development Program. In addition, she has given guest lectures at the Hasso Plattner Institute of Design (the "d.school") and the Career Development Center at Stanford, and she has been featured in leading publications such as *Fast Company*, *Forbes*, and *Women's Health*.

Danielle started her career as a Teach For America corps member, and she later served as a mentor and advisor for Global Leadership Adventures (GLA), an international leadership development and service program. In addition to teaching in the United States, she has taught in Brazil, China, Costa Rica, and South Africa. She is a member of the International Leadership Association, the Association for Practical and Professional Ethics, and the National Association for Female Executives, and she is a certified fitness instructor. In her spare time, she enjoys trail running, yoga, snorkeling, climbing, reading (good) fiction, and creating mixed media art.

Danielle's TEDx talk, "Reimagining Leadership for the 21st Century," can be viewed at www.youtube.com/watch?v=6sjrMPwT0tA.